I0510204

REAL ESTATE MARKETING AND EFFECTIVE COMMUNICATION

2 BOOKS IN 1

to convey effective communication
in real estate marketing through
social networks, negotiations and
personal relationship

DIEGO DE GIOVANNI

TABLE OF CONTENTS

THE COMPLETE GUIDE TO REAL ESTATE MARKETING

DIEGO DE GIOVANNI

DEDICATION

I want to dedicate this book to all the people who have supported me by my side and encouraged me in these twenty years of experience.
And then of course as always the biggest dedication goes to my family, my partner Alessia and my daughter Alice.

Introduction

Real estate is the property, land, buildings, air rights above the land and underground rights underneath including uncultivated flora and fauna, farmed crops and livestock, water and mineral deposits.The expression real estate means real, or physical, property. "Real" comes from the Latin root res, or things. Others say it is from the Latin word rex, meaning "royal," since kings used to own all land inside their kingdoms.

Real estate is a tangible asset and a form of real property. Real property includes land, buildings as well as other improvements, in addition to the rights of good use and enjoyment of that land and all sorts of its improvements. Renters and leaseholders might have rights to inhabit land or buildings that are considered an integral part of their estate, but these rights themselves are not, strictly speaking, considered real estate.

Real property is not the same as and may not to ever be mistaken for personal property. Personal property includes intangible assets like investments, along with tangible assets such as for example furniture and fixtures like a dishwasher. Also, even renters may claim areas of a property as personal property, provided you bought and installed the property using the lessor's permission.

CATEGORIES OF REAL ESTATE

Real estate have different categories which we have looked into in this book, the categories include;

- Residential Real Estate
- Commercial Real Estate
- Industrial Real Estate
- Land

Residential Real Estate

Residential real estate includes undeveloped land, houses, condominiums, and town houses. The structures might be single-family or multi-family dwellings and could be owner occupied or rental properties.

Within the 2019 edition of its annual home-value analysis, the real estate website Zillow estimated the full total worth of all U.S. homes in 2018 was $33.3 trillion, 71% more than the country's gross domestic product (GDP) of $19.4 trillion at that time. Homeownership, also called owner-occupancy, is one of common type's of real estate investment in america. In line with the National Multifamily Housing Council (NMHC), roughly two-thirds of residents own their home. Often, these owners have financed the acquisition by taking out a mortgage loan, when the property will act as collateral when it comes to debt.

Individuals shopping for home mortgages to assist them to realize the dream of property ownership are faced with many different options. Mortgages can charge either fixed-rate or variable-rate interest. Fixed-rate mortgages generally have higher interest rates than variable-rate mortgages, which could make them higher priced within the short run. Fixed-rate loans cost more for the short term as they are protected from future rate of interest increases.

Banks publish amortization schedules that show simply how much of a borrower's monthly obligations head to paying off interest versus how much goes to paying down the principal of the loan. Balloon loans are mortgages that do not fully amortize reduce to zero over time. Instead, the borrower pays interest for a group period, 5 years as an example, and then must pay the remaining associated with loan in a balloon payment at the end of the expression.

Also, mortgages go along with heavy costs that include transaction fees and taxes. These additional expenses in many cases are rolled in to the loan. Once potential homeowners' have proven their eligibility and secured a mortgage from a bank or any other lender, they have to complete additional steps to make sure the property is legally on the market plus in good shape.

Residential Real Estate also Includes both new construction and resale homes. The most common category is single-family homes. There are condominiums, co-ops, townhouses, duplexes, triple-deckers, *q*uadplexes, high-value homes, multi-generational and vacation homes.

Commercial Real Estate

Commercial real estate includes non residential structures such as for instance office buildings, warehouses, and retail buildings. These buildings could be free standing or in shopping malls.

Commercial real estate is used for commerce and includes anything from strip malls and free standing restaurants to office buildings and skyscrapers. It is often distinguished from industrial real estate, which is practical space utilized in the manufacturing of products.

Buying or leasing real estate for commercial purposes is extremely not the same as buying a house or even buying residential real estate. Commercial leases are generally longer than residential leases. Commercial real estate returns are derived from their profitability per s*q*uare foot, unlike structures intended to be private residences. Moreover, lenders may necessitate a more substantial down payment on home financing for commercial real estate then what exactly is needed for a residence.

Commercial real estate also Includes shopping malls and strip malls, medical and educational buildings, hotels and offices. Apartment buildings in many cases are considered commercial, even though they've been utilized for residences. Which is since they are owned to produce income.

Industrial Real Estate

Industrial real estate includes factories, business parks, mines, and farms. These properties usually are larger in size and locations can include access to transportation hubs such as for instance rail lines and harbors.

This includes manufacturing buildings and property, as well as warehouses. The buildings may be used for research, production, storage and distribution of products. Some buildings that distribute goods are considered commercial real estate. The classification is important due to the fact zoning, construction and sales are handled differently.

Land

Includes land that is vacant working farms and ranches. The subcategories within vacant land include undeveloped, early development or reuse, subdivision and site assembly.

REAL ESTATE INDUSTRY

Real estate also relates to producing, buying and selling real estate. Real estate affects the U.S. economy when you're a crucial driver of economic growth.

Construction of brand new buildings is an element of gross domestic product. It offers both residential, commercial, and industrial buildings. In 2018, real estate construction contributed $1.15 trillion to the nation's economic output. That is 6.2 percent of U.S. gross domestic product. It is more than the $1.13 trillion in 2017, but nevertheless not as much as the 2006 peak of $1.19 trillion. During those times, real estate construction was a hefty 8.9 percent element of GDP.

New house building is a critical category. It offers construction of single-family homes, town houses and condominiums. The National Association of Home Builders provides monthly data on home sales and average prices. The info on new house sales is a leading economic indicator. It signals the way the housing industry can do in nine months. That's how long it will require to construct new homes. The NAHB also reports new home starts, those would be the quantity of home construction projects on which ground is broken.

Real estate professionals assist homeowners, businesses and investors buy and sell all four types of properties. The industry is usually divided up into specialists that focus using one of this types.

Sellers' agents help find buyers through either the Multiple Listing Service or their professional contacts. They price your premises, using comparative listings of recently sold properties known as "comps". The will allow you to spruce up your property therefore it can look its best to customers. They help in negotiations using the buyer, assisting you to get the highest price possible. Listed here are more sellers' agent services.

Buyers' agents provide similar services for the home purchaser. They know the local market. That means they are able to find a property that meets your most significant criteria. Additionally they compare prices, called "doing comps." It allows them to guide you to areas that are affordable. Buyers' agents negotiate for you personally, pointing out reasons why the vendor should accept a lower life expectancy price. They assistance with the legalities for the process, including title search, inspection and financing.

REAL ESTATE INVESTING

Everyone who buys or sells a property engages in real estate investing. This means you have to consider several factors. Will the home increase in value whilst you live in it? If you get a home loan, how will future interest rates and taxes affect you?

Many individuals do this well with investing within their homes they wish to buy and sell homes as a business. There are numerous methods to accomplish that. First, you can easily flip a home. That's where you get a home to enhance then sell it. Lots of people own several homes and rent them out. Others use Airbnb as a convenient way to rent out all or section of their homes. It is possible to rent vacation homes using VRBO or Home Away.

You are able to invest in housing without buying a house. You should buy stocks of homebuilders. Their stock prices rise and fall with all the housing industry. Another way is by using Real Estate Investment Trusts, called REITS. They are investments in commercial real estate. Their stock prices lag behind trends in residential real estate by a few years.

Unlike other investments, real estate is dramatically affected by its surroundings and immediate geographic area. Hence the well-known real-estate maxim "location, location, location." Except for a severe national recession or depression, residential real estate values, in particular, are affected primarily by local factors. Such factors include the area's employment rate, the area economy, crime rates, transportation facilities, quality of schools, municipal services, and property taxes.

You will find key variations in residential and commercial real estate investments. From the one hand, residential real estate is generally less costly and smaller than commercial real estate, and so it is more affordable for the small investor.

On the other hand, commercial real estate is often times more valuable per sq ft, and its leases are longer, which theoretically ensures a far more predictable income stream. With greater revenue comes greater responsibility. Commercial rental real estate is more heavily regulated than residential real estate, and these regulations may vary not merely from nation to nation and state by state but additionally by county and city. Even within cities, zoning regulations add a layer of unwanted complexity to commercial real estate investments.

There is increased risk of tenant turnover in commercial rental agreements. In the event that lessee's business design is bad, their product is unattractive, or they truly are poor managers, they might file for bankruptcy. The business failure can abruptly stop expensive real estate from generating revenue.

Moreover, just like property can appreciate, it can also depreciate. Once-hot retail locations have been proven to decay into rotten shopping malls and dead malls.

Pros
- Offers steady income
- Offers capital appreciation
- Diversifies portfolio
- Can be bought with leverage

Cons
- Is usually illiquid
- Influenced by highly local factors
- Requires big initial capital outlay
- May require active management, expertise

Tips for proper Investment

Many people has jump into the property investment bandwagon. In the past, buying a property for the true purpose of selling in a nutshell term was definitely tempting and possible. To date, buying a residential property and selling it in a short time is definitely harder as compared to decades ago. Simply because the house market has slowed down significantly and property prices no longer rise as much as a result of government's measure to cool off the market.

Location

First of all, do keep in mind location plays a crucial role with regards to property investment. The positioning you like will have an effect on the price plus the potential growth in the near future.

How do you define "good location"? Look at the location of the property. May be the property located at a spot that is ideal to live in? Is the location convenient? Does the area have easy option of public transport and amenities? Are there any public transportations such as train station nearby? What are the education institutions within the vicinities? These are all the factors which will affect and determine the buying price of the property and the rental yield.

On a side note, you should stay close to your home investment if you intend to rent it out. This will save you from plenty of hassle when it comes to handling tenant complaints and maintenance.

Real Estate Agent

Finding the right real estate agent is essential as well. A beneficial real estate agent could save you from hassles and stress as they begin to be the anyone to handle any property related matters on your behalf. All things considered, they truly are real estate professionals with professional expertise that you don't have. Furthermore, they definitely have significantly more experience than you are doing when it comes to handling property related matters.

If you're looking for the best property to buy, tell your real estate agent according to your preferences and they will perform some rest to find you an ideal property with favorable price. If you should be about to rent out your home, they're going to then enable you to seek out potential tenants. With all the right real estate agent, it is possible to definitely sell out or rent out your home much easier and far **q**uicker.

Choosing the best loan

Once we know that properties fit in with illi**q**uid assets, it may never be a great idea to place all your valuable money in properties. You will need to understand that the entire process of selling a house just isn't easy. It might take approximate 6 months to a year, or more to sell off the property. Even so, the purchase price that you will be selling the house is probably not the best price. Hence, it is advisable to opt for a home loan to finance your investment. With so many loans offered by different banks, it is crucial for you yourself to educate yourself on the loans available. Find out of the difference between interest levels, prepayment penalties and settlement cost offered by different banks. Make sure you choose the loan that best you prefer.

In addition, you are able to make use of the money you can get from your own rental income to fund your monthly mortgage instalments. In order to make a profit from renting out your property, the ideal instalment is approximately 60% for the rental income you receive.

Types of property

There are lots of types of property available, such as for example condominiums, apartments and landed properties. You will need to select the right variety of property according to your re**q**uirements. Landed properties are often more costly than condominium units or apartment units. However, landed properties appreciate more in value in comparison with apartments. That said, you need to invest in landed property, even just one storey house is going to do, because it will provide you with more advantages ultimately.

This however does not mean apartments are not a worthy investment. Apartments or condominiums are more suited to renting. In addition, it really is more appealing to very first time property buyers due to the fact price is relatively cheaper than landed properties. Be sure you always stay within your budget.

Last but most certainly not least, do take into account on the types of property you spend money on, in terms of leasehold property or freehold property. Leasehold property has a limited leasing period (normally 99 years) which is renewable. As for freehold property, it really is a residential property with no leasing period. This means, the house is yours forever.

property investment isn't as difficult because it seems. It might appear daunting but the return is definitely worth the time and effort and money which you have call at, provided you made it happen the right way. Make sure you research your facts and plan ahead before buying properties for investment purpose to avoid getting into financial debts. All things considered, it really is an investment that costs a lot and does not come cheap.

HOW TO PROFIT FROM REAL ESTATE

One could invest in real estate directly by purchasing actual properties or parcels of land; or indirectly, by buying shares in publicly traded real estate investment trusts (REITs) or mortgage-backed securities (MBS). The indirect investment methods may offer less return and less control, but they are vastly more liquid than owning physical real estate and don't require in-depth familiarity with the real estate business.

Investing directly in real estate leads to profits or losses

through two avenues, which may haven't changed in centuries:
- •Revenue from rent or leases
- •Appreciation associated with real estate's value

Appreciation

Appreciation is achieved through different means, but the boost in a property's value isn't realized until the owner sells his house. Another way to comprehend profit is to refinance the mortgage. Raw and undeveloped land, like the territory right outside a city's borders, supplies the biggest potential for construction, enhancement, and profit. Appreciation can also result from discovering valuable materials or natural resources on a plot of land, like striking oil. Also, an increase in the market values of the area all over land you possess.

As a neighborhood grows and develops, property values have a tendency to climb. The gentrification of urban neighborhoods in some American cities during the last few decades has often led to a dramatic increase in real estate prices. Scarcity also can may play a role in the worth of real estate holdings. If a whole lot is the last of the size or kind in a prestigious area or one where such lots rarely become available it gains in marketability.

Income

Income from real estate comes in many forms. The greatest generator may be the rent paid on land already progressed into residential or commercial properties. However, companies will even pay royalties for natural resource discoveries on raw land. Also, they could pay to build structures upon it, like cell towers or pipelines.

Income can also come from indirect real estate investments. In a REIT, the owner of multiple properties sells shares to investors and passes along rental income by means of distributions. Similarly, in an MBS, the interest and principal payments from a pool of mortgages are collected and passed through to investors.

Both REITs and MBS investment products trade like stocks, with real estate acting as their underlying security.

So, they could offer capital appreciation could be the shares gain in market value.

HOME STATISTICS IN RELATION TO REAL ESTATE

Statistics about new home construction are important leading economic indicators. This means they are going to give you an advance notice on the future associated with housing market.

All these indicators tells just a little different story concerning the health for the homebuilding industry. For instance, say home starts are steady, but housing starts decline. That will take a toll on home sales. Many buyers might not desire to wait more than a year. Moreover it means there's a shortage of lumber, concrete, or construction workers. Those shortages could drive up costs, and sales prices. That could further decrease need for new homes.

If mortgages are declining, the homebuilder will end up with a listing of unsold homes for sale. In addition it means demand is high, but homeowners can not get mortgages. Rising home starts may appear like an indication of housing strength. But it may be a negative sign. Declining home closings mean the housing market is weak.

The brand new home sale is the initial step in a nine to twelve-month process. If new house sales pick up, then you definitely know closings will boost in about a year. However, all of the remaining three steps should be completed.

A fresh home sales occurs when the buyer signs the paperwork and provides the homebuilder a deposit. That's since most new homes are not constructed until there is a buyer. The exceptions are spec homes which can be used as model homes. The Census Bureau releases monthly estimates of the latest home sales. They are given as an annual rate.

2 months following the paperwork is signed, your local housing regulators grant the permit. It is an early on indicator, not always accurate. Builders can go bankrupt and do not build the permitted units. They could replace the number of units built in a multi-family. In fact, 22.5 percent of multi-family permits aren't built, or are changed to single-family units. Finally, developers often receive permits for a large percentage of a complex that could take months and month to build.

90 days later is the new house start. It occurs when the builder breaks ground. The National Association of Home Builders reports with this monthly. It's very accurate since the new home start only takes place when the builder is confident enough to break ground.

Six to nine months later could be the closing. The homebuyer must receive home financing before the home can close. If the homebuyer does not *q*ualify, your house remains in inventory. If this statistic is lower than the home sale figure, it means this new real estate market will *q*uickly slow down. There are too many homes being built, rather than enough *q*ualified home buyers. It may also mean builders will begin lowering prices to clear their inventories. Fannie Mae releases the report on all mortgages.

You will find three other important indicators to view.

Inventory - This is the total of homes that are offered for sale, but unsold. The NAHB reports this monthly.

Months of Supply this is one way many months it can decide to try sell all the houses in inventory. It is on the basis of the sales rate and inventory. The NAHB also reports this monthly.

Sales Prices - The Census Bureau reports on both the median and average new house sales price.

REAL ESTATE WHOLESALING

Real estate wholesaling generally seems to be growing in visibility. How exactly does it work?

Flipping houses happens to be ever more popular in modern times. Wholesaling is a form of house flipping, and may even prove to be a key strategy more investors will embrace into the developing housing market. So, so how exactly does it work? Exactly what are the benefits? What role might real estate agents play in the process?

The Idea

Many people have trouble with new concepts like wholesaling real estate, however the basic idea has been a typical section of our economy and shopping habits for a long time. Probably the most notable examples of this are Walmart, Costco, and Amazon.

Walmart has generated a huge footprint on its ability to buy inventory in large volume at affordable prices and sell that inventory at a profit. It's businesses like these and their logistics which have also helped legendary investors like Warren Buffett get to be the richest people on earth. Grocery and consumer goods wholesaler Costco is continuing to grow even bigger than Walmart in certain areas, grossing almost $120B a year ago. Amazon has established a digital platform which essentially wholesales almost everything you can ever are interested to buy.

How It Operates

Real estate wholesaling works much like any other kind of wholesaling. The theory is to purchase properties low, and sell for a profit to another end buyer. Most commonly, this is done by targeting discounted or undervalued properties, and then flipping them to rehabbers or rental property investors. Some wholesalers flip their properties to regular retail buyers, others focus on bulk portfolio deals.

Some wholesalers buy and sell properties for cash. Others use short term financing like credit lines, hard money, or transactional funding. Others concentrate on simply securing and assigning, or 'flipping' contracts.

Wholesaling real estate differs from traditional fixing and flipping of houses in that these investors generally don't do any rehab work. They purchase and sell as-is. Though some may do minor cleaning up, make cosmetic improvements, or 'prehab' to create on a clean slate for the next buyer.

The Benefits of Wholesale Investing in Real Estate

Among the list of top reasons investors choose this owning a home strategy include:
- One of the easiest real estate strategies to master
- Speed of getting in, out, and paid
- No handyman or construction experience needed
- Short holdings times which reduce risk and costs
- High profit margins
- Can work in up and down markets
-

The Legal Debates

There are often debates about the legality of flipping and wholesaling houses. Some argue that wholesaling is illegal. Often that is because of misconceptions concerning the strategy. Various other cases it is a matter of not conducting activities which require a license, in the event that you don't get one. It's important that all individual do their research, know their local laws, and consult legal counsel and licensed professionals for guidance. Make certain you stick to the law and wholesaling isn't only legal, but highly profitable as well.

House Flipping Statistics

RealtyTrac tracks homes which are bought and sold within 12 months, and so are considered flips. Wholesale properties certainly are categorized as this category. To demonstrate the possibility for this strategy the latest stats through the annual House Flipping Report show the following:

- 193,009 houses were flipped this past year
- Almost 6% of all house and condo sales just last year were flips
- 126,256 individuals and business entities flipped houses this past year
- The typical house flipping gross profit in 2016 was $62,624
- More than 11 cities have average profits of over $100,000
- The average ROI is 49.2%
- 9 cities posted flipping profits above 75% just last year
- Wholesaling MLS Properties

You'll find so many methods to find wholesale property deals. Including:

- Newspaper ads
- Craigslist
- Foreclosure auctions
- Bank REOs
- Your very own website
- Social media marketing
- The MLS

Some real estate trainers focus on more guerrilla

marketing methods of finding deals. Others find they can build a fantastic pipeline of business from Realtors and properties on the Multiple Listing Service. This might save time and costs, and make certain consistency in volume, while benefiting from the legal protection of employing an authorized agent. Built with the right information, good negotiation skills, in accordance with some remarketing help investors can leverage the incredible number of properties into the MLS and from the other sources, to construct a proper business that has the potential for making millions of dollars a year.

Find a real estate agent familiar with Real Estate Wholesaling on UpNest!

The numbers recorded by RealtyTrac plus the popularity of top wholesaling brands suggest this could be a profitable strategy for others. There are clear advantages of wholesaling for people who are simply getting started, with a great amount of growth and long term potential as well. There are a variety of ways to get started, including reaching out to local real estate agents for help negotiating MLS properties, which could also help investors stick to just the right region of the law. Use UpNest for connecting with top agents in your area, and begin growing your income with real estate wholesaling today!

BEING A REAL ESTATE AGENT

The actual estate agent could be the workhorse associated with industry. He's a salesman one moment, a buyer's advocate the following; he's an analyst, an auctioneer, a consultant, a negotiator, and a marketer; he occasionally performs the services of an appraiser, a clerk, and a loan officer; he accommodates his clients on nights and weekends, and frequently works well beyond forty hours per week.

Basically, a real estate agent does a little of everything, as well as for that, he's paid a modest commission (provided, of course, that he closes the offer). It's no wonder, then, that a lot of agents cycle inside and outside associated with the industry. It's also no wonder that demand for their services remains high even yet in a slow market.

Tips to Become a Good Real Estate Agent

Real estate is a small business

In recent years we've seen some new trends when it comes to the consumer's relationship with the realtor industry. A lot more than ever before, the typical average person has access to the kinds of statistics, market analyses, technology, and expert opinions which were previously reserved for people who actively made their living as an agent or broker.

Prior to the Internet, a lot of these records would only exist within the mouths of working agents or in agent licensure textbooks. Consumers had little importance of these records simply because they trusted their real estate professional to learn it.

Today, Realtors are blabbing throughout the blogosphere, even making a buck by telling consumers simple tips to do their jobs. "How to generate income in Real Estate: Five Easy Steps." "Flipping Homes for Fun and Profit." Consequently, some appear to think about becoming a realtor like using up an interest, something to occupy your recovery time and get you quick cash at exactly the same time.

But the majority hobbies are cheap, and also the expensive ones are about the sheer enjoyment associated with the activity. With a hobby, you're allowed to be careless since you don't have anything to get rid of. Neglect your herb garden for a couple days? No big deal. Don't play your guitar per month? It'll still be there whenever your fingers obtain the itch.

Real estate, on the other hand, is a small business. It's about money, so when the marketplace has revealed in the last several years, when you are getting careless in real estate, you stand to reduce plenty of it. As a real estate agent, you're an independent contractor, which means it's up to you to manage your own business. Any agent who picks up your slack isn't handing it back once again to you.

Finally, hobbies are personal, while real estate is professional. Typically, only the individuals with whom you decide to share your hobbies know about them, which means they don't have a massive effect on your public image.

But since your conduct as a real estate agent takes place when you look at the professional world, it has much an extended paper trail. Just about anybody can know about it. Fail to satisfy a customer, and you're telling her and everybody she knows that you're unreliable—which may have serious ramifications for other regions of your life.

None for this means you ought ton't enjoy being employed as a Realtor. Quite the opposite, you're not likely to reach your goals in the event that you don't.

Nevertheless the best agents are those who marry the pleasure they get from their work to a knowledge that it's, well, work.

Leads and listings, yet not necessarily in that order

It doesn't matter what business you're in, selling is hard. As an agent, however, the challenge is even greater because repeat customers are few and far in between.

Homes, most likely, are not electronics or fashion items. They're not built to be replaced after a year, nor do they become obsolete. People buy homes with the intention of staying put. In a perfect world, your clients won't need you again for a long time.

True, unforeseen circumstances require visitors to move, and based on the latest census, 69.3 percent of most movers stayed within the same county, which means significantly more than two-thirds of movers might be returning to the same Realtor. Nevertheless, altogether only 12.5 percent of the U.S. population changed residences this season. That's a small increase since 2008, but in general, this share has decreased by about 50 % because the late 1940s.

Furthermore, these statistics vary widely depending on where you live. About 14.7 percent of Westerners moved in 2010, but that does you no good in the event that you operate in the Northeast, where only 8.3 percent did exactly the same.

So how do you grow your organization when interest in the services you provide is bound? By working both sides associated with the real estate equation. Several years ago, agents worked exclusively with sellers, listing their properties for sale and rent. In those days, your task would be to have the word out about a seller's property and attract buyers. The more listings you had, the higher off you had been.

Today, however, it's also common to work with the

buyer. In this scenario, success is all about leads, folks who are thinking about buying a home. As soon as you've found a lead, your job is always to turn him from a prospect to a customer by helping him secure the house he'd prefer to rent or purchase.

This usually means you're a matchmaker, connecting buyers with listings your agency already has. You might like to be an advocate, helping them browse someone else's listings. In either case, the arrangement is simply exactly the same: agents use their experience to ensure buyers don't get screwed. In the place of selling a property, you're selling your expertise.

So which can be more important, leads or listings? That will depend on where you are. But whatever the figures, it's vital to keep a close eye on both. In an arduous market and a changing industry, the best way to success for an agent is to be adaptable and prepared to work with sellers and buyers. Concentrate solely on a single, and you'll find yourself struggling maintain your business afloat.

Relationships are everything

Every agent is glued to his iPhone or laptop screen these days. However, it is important to remember on the reverse side of all those zeroes and ones are real people, and they're the ones who keep your business going.

Relationships are your bread and butter and when we say that, we're not talking the little dinner rolls you fill up on before your meal arrives.

To know simple tips to maximize your relationships as a realtor, start by asking the basic questions: that do you realize, and that knows you? The answers will go far in revealing the extent of one's sphere of influence, the collection of people for whom you as well as your business have weight. The more your sphere of influence, the greater amount of of a magnet you then become for prospects and the better your chances of turning them into customers.

The cliché goes that real estate is about location. That isn't pretty much inventory: it's about involvement. To optimize your online business, you need to participate in your community. Join your local Realtor's association. Coach just a little league team. Attend town government meetings. Get exposure within the flesh, and make sure people know what you do.

By showing you're enthusiastic about the life span of one's community, you demonstrate that you have an individual stake in every the business enterprise you are doing as a real estate agent. You should also treat everyone you meet up with the same courtesy and attention, no matter who they are or what they can perform for you personally after all, you will never know who may become a person.

Knowing and being known by as many folks that you can is essential, specially when there aren't lots of prospects to go around. But while $q$uantity is great, $q$uality is even better. Visibility is great, but if your only goal is to obtain everyone and anyone from the hook, knowing everybody in the city will really work against you. Your reputation in your community greatly influences your trade. People obviously want to work with agents they trust.

The essential sustainable business design is just one by which your transactions with other people are often mutually beneficial. Real estate, is approximately earning profits; but focus too much on your profit margins, and you'll find you've got fewer and fewer customers looking to hand theirs over.

Finally, as soon as you've established your relationships, it's imperative to have them up, whether or not they're causing you to money right now. Follow through with recent customers to see how they're settling in. Distribute a message newsletter to all your clients. Send personalized notes and birthday cards. Use social media marketing and continue maintaining a presence online. If you feel as you haven't spoken to a vintage customer in a little while, send them a contact to in$q$uire of how they're doing. The gesture only takes one to three minutes, and it will pay huge dividends in the end.

Each contact you make has a value, and every customer has an eternity value. Lose contact with your prospects, leads and customers, and you'll be squandering your greatest asset.

Develop a personality.

It's often said that as a salesman, you're not just selling your product or service: you're selling yourself. That's why as an agent, it's important to develop a personality.

We're not saying you don't get one: we're just suggesting that you lean into it. Whether you're a pet lover, a motorcycle enthusiast, a foodie or an internet gamer, don't hide your personality: embrace it. You're in real estate so, for God's sake, be real. Your personality fosters relationships, which builds your reputation, which generates leads. You will get the picture.

Getting involved in the life of a community helps create your relationships, but it's important that the involvement be in line with who you are as an individual. Enthusiasm is difficult to fake, so if something you say or do doesn't ring true to you personally, individuals will pick up on it.

If you're an enthusiastic carnivore, for instance, shopping for leads at an ASPCA meeting probably is not a beneficial idea and in fact, it might cause both the individuals you meet together with people you are already aware to consider you as a hypocrite.

Instead, you're better off finding opportunities to broadcast yourself to people who have that you have common ground. In terms of those opportunities go, some say it's safer to keep politics and religion out of business, and perhaps those people are right. But politics and religion build strong communities, and according to what your location is, getting involved may have huge benefits. As well, it's important for you to decide what you're comfortable wearing on the sleeve.

We're speaking about work here, therefore it's

important to see personality in an expert context. As a whole, moderation and a sense of boundaries are keys to success. Come on too strong or get too personal in your dealings with clients, and you might end up alienating more people than you relate solely to.

Instead, let customers function as the ones to open your responsibility, and they'll often be happier for it after all, many people enjoy speaking about themselves more than anything else.

THINGS TO DO BEFORE STARTING A REAL ESTATE CAREER

So you're thinking about becoming a realtor? A real estate career is an exciting opportunity that can introduce you to many interesting people and if you work smart can provide a comfortable income. However, there are many things for you yourself to consider and actions to do before beginning the new pursuit.

Here are some the activities to do before launching your real estate career.

Be Honest with Yourself.

This is probably the most important item regarding the list. Essentially, ask yourself (and answer) "what is my motivation?"

If you're driven by the lure of easy money, STOP NOW. It's quite difficult and it also takes a lot of time and effort. The money can come only if you work smart and put forth the time and effort.

If you should be not scared of hard work, enjoy meeting new people and providing a site to others then keep on reading! This can be for your needs.

Real Estate is part marketing, part sales, part entrepreneurship, and a big part customer service. So think through each one of these while making sure you may be willing to do them all, particularly the customer support part.

Will you be good with change? This really is a fast paced business and tools associated with trade are changing rapidly. One minute our company is using laptops and also the next we have been showing homes on tablets. MLS systems are changing quickly as well so we all have to be able to adapt easily to new software and websites. Also, laws are changing and we also must stay as much as date and know the way they impact us and our clients.

Interview Current Real Estate Professionals.

This follows no. 1 very closely. I recommend which you interview several real estate agents to understand the advantages and cons regarding the job. Don't just interview the top agents and/or your real estate professional friends. It is advisable to interview agents at different points inside their career – established agents and ones getting started. Check out *q*uestions to think about asking them:
- What exactly are their daily and weekly routines?
- What do they love and hate about their jobs?

•What advice would they give to new agents?

•What do they consider to end up being the most important quality in a great agent?

•What are the common pitfalls to prevent when getting started?

•How important may be the role of technology for the real estate agent?

Once you've your entire questions answered, reflect back in the responses and write a list for the common factors that were mentioned over the interviewees. Arrive at your personal conclusion, and if need be revisit number one on the list to make sure this career is for you.

Know how exactly to Budget and take action.

Taking care of a commission can be very rough for folks who are used to getting regular paychecks. You really must be diligent with your budgeting and savings to avoid adding financial stress on top of the already stressful task of starting an innovative new career. Personal Budgeting is key for longevity as a commissioned sales person.

Consider a Second Source of Income

This may actually serve a couple of purposes.

First, it could relieve financial stress from focusing on commission and never deplete your savings account (and also maybe add to it).

Second, your other job can provide a fantastic source of potential clients and expand your sphere of influence. You should be careful with promoting yourself and new career in excess. Some employer's may frown at this.

Start Building your Database of Contacts

It's never too early to start out compiling a listing of people who you may reach out to and let them know that you're a brand new real estate professional.

Be sure to include as much associated with the following as you can:
- Full Name
- Email
- Home Address
- Home and Mobile Telephone Numbers
- Birth Dates
- List of Family Relations
- Employer and Occupation

Treat this as a small business (since it is!)

When you are getting your real estate license and interviewing agents and firms, you should keep track of your mileage and other expenses. Talk to your tax preparer about allowable expenses and start to trace them accordingly.

Write A Business Strategy. There are several books and resources on the Internet to help with this effort. Planning is extremely important and staying with your plan will assist you to remain on track to earning a profit. Note: you will probably need to modify your first few plans as you receive the hang of the expenses and client conversion ratios so don't be too much on yourself when you have to tweak your plan.

Learn through the Best

There are lots of books and Internet tools offered by top agents that are meant to inspire and teach. The best may be the Millionaire real estate professional by Gary Keller (of Keller Williams). I look at this book when I was initially getting started and can still pick it up whenever I need only a little kick start.

Research the greatest Broker Firm for you.

This can be among the final and vital pieces to possess set up before starting your new career.

You need to try to find a company that has excellent online tools and offers classes and/or mentorships to new agents.

It should be a good fit together with your personality. You will find office politics EVERYWHERE so be sure you are comfortable in your new environment.

Remember through your conversations/ interviews you are interviewing them as well. This is simply not a job interview so do not be nervous. As a realtor you're in business for yourself and you also need to find an excellent partner. The best broker firm could be the partner that will help reach your goals.

Arrive at Know your Neighborhood and Surrounding Area.

It's never prematurily to start looking around, visiting open houses and looking at the costs in your market. Here are a few facts to consider:

•Know the inventory of homes in your selected market.

•Start compiling a list of parks and activities in the region.

Have a go at town meetings and perhaps serve on a committee. This is where you are going to hear information first as well as have the ability to expand your contact database.

You are not only selling homes but also neighborhoods so go ahead and begin pulling together marketing material. The Chamber of Commerce might be able to provide some useful resources.

Get Licensed.

Every state has it is own set of requirements to be a licensed real estate professional. Please read the map I've put together and click in your state to visit your state educational requirements. Math is often a sticking point for some agents during the exam so I've written several

Real Estate Math posts to greatly help aspiring real estate professionals.

STARTING A REAL ESTATE BUSINESS

Starting a real estate business requires lots of work, training and time. Although the laws vary in each state, starting an actual estate business is normally a three-step process that can take at the very least couple of years. Before beginning your personal company, you need to become a licensed real estate broker, and before becoming a broker, you truly must be a licensed sales agent.

Planning

Whether you're starting a genuine estate business, a large part coffee shop, or an organization that manufactures rocket parts, it's smart to write a business plan. Business planning makes you more successful it is been scientifically proven!

Not only can working through the planning process prompt you to definitely think of essential things like how you're positioned to contend with similar businesses, and exactly how much cash you'll want to actually get started, it will also allow you to validate your idea and get into a habit of setting goals and milestones.

Based on real estate investor Eric Bowlin, the purpose of a business plan is twofold. He says, "First, it provides you a method to formalize your targets and direction. More to the point, it really is a document that you could provide to lenders or investors to clearly illustrate not just your direction but what your location is and how you've got there." During the planning process, Eric got a lot of great advice from an area small company Development Center.

When you haven't had any experience in the actual estate industry, it's smart to get advice from anyone who has. Real estate agent Jamal Asskoumi of Castle Smart says, "If you yourself are in a roundabout way involved in real estate, then it's better to find someone who is, in the planning stage. They'll know far more of the do's and dont's."

Of course, you might always go down the route of taking formal courses on the topic, or reading the best books.

Market research and idea validation

How do you know you've got a thought that will work? How will you know you've picked a distinct segment into the real estate market that truly has a target audience? How will you work out how to position yourself through this niche?

These *q*uestions and many more like them could be answered within the initial market research phase. By conducting both primary and secondary marketing research, you give yourself a broader idea of set up target audience you've picked is valuable enough to pursue.

Needless to say, there's no one-fits-all method of figuring out what niche you're best served to help and the selection of responses we got from real estate agents across the United States is proof of that.

Do general market trends early

Finding the time to do your market research early may also help you save both time and money. Michelle Stansbury, an agent at Bluegrass Partners Trust Realty says, "My first year was lots of fumbling around figuring out what didn't work. My second year I tripled my business."

Do market research to assess your personal skills

Brad Pauly, who owns Pauly Presley Realty, took exactly the same learning from your errors approach however for him, it had been a great way to figure out his own strengths and weaknesses. "I figured out my target audience through trial and error," he says. "When I started in the industry, I wouldn't turn away any business! Once I realized my strong suits, I centered on them. Four years when I was licensed, I obtained my broker's license and created the company we have today."

If you're not clear on your own personal strengths and weaknesses, conducting a SWOT analysis will allow you to figure them out.

Get some good real-world experience or find a mentor

If you're a doer first, another approach to market research is to simply get in there and start doing things. A lot of people don't have the excess time or money to work on this, however if you do, good for you, it's as valid a way as any. Morgan Franklin, an authorized real estate agent based out of Lexington, Kentucky, says, "I became confident [my idea] would definitely work because I had already developed enough business to pay most of my startup expenses before I took my real estate exam."

However, Morgan did spend some time employed by a real estate attorney so he previously a bit of know-how before diving in. "If you've got no experience, I would strongly urge a fresh agent to find a mentor to work with for the first couple of years," he suggests. If you haven't had much exposure to the industry, going the "mentor" route is a great idea.

Having said that, Morgan did do a fair bit of research himself. When asked how he figured out who his target audience was, he responded, "I looked over the volume of sales in my city, from the property valuation administrator, after which looked for the 'sweet spot.' That is where the majority of the amount of transactions was occurring. After that, I aimed when it comes to top end of the group."

Cheryl Julcher, the Managing Broker at Yellow Brick Properties, did her general market trends, but also decided to begin in an area she felt passionate about. "Here at Yellow Brick, many of us are about healthy, safe, comfortable, and smart homes eco-conscious and sustainable housing," she explains.

"We went with this passion, which is what I would advise you to do," says Cheryl. "Go with all the market sector millennials, empty nesters, etc. that you care about the essential and therefore are most experienced in."

When you have strong feelings about a specific sector, odds are it is a great spot to at the very least start doing all of your researching the market.

Branding

Branding is important for businesses of each size. If you've got a memorable brand, it is better to build credibility, look bigger than you are, attract customers, as well as in general end up being the first person or company people think about.

According to branding expert Sara Conte of Brand Genie, "Although it is possible to influence your brand through well-designed logos, hilarious ad campaigns, carefully crafted pr announcements, or super-friendly service, ultimately, your brand is exactly what the surface world says it really is."

Essentially, your reputation is the brand.

Branding tip 1: Your reputation is perhaps all down seriously to your relationships

Real estate agent Jamal Asskoumi, of Castle Smart, knows this well; not merely does he have confidence in the necessity of setting yourself apart from the competition, but also into the need for your relationships together with your clients.

"When branding in real estate, make an effort to allow it to be as personal as you can. That is a company which relies heavily on interaction and building relationships. Ensure your business exudes the same welcoming smile you have."

Be someone people would you like to align themselves with. You may be the brand, all things considered.

Realtor Tim Frie takes this idea a step further. He says, "Building a reputation is much more important than building a brand in real estate...plus, building a reputation is easier than constructing a brandname."

Branding tip 2: Provide value and present people what they need

Reputation and authenticity appear to go in conjunction in real estate. Michael Kelczewski a realtor for Brandywine Fine Properties Sotheby's International, feels that folks can sense non-verbal cues and behavior patterns. As a result, there's much less that may go wrong if you behave authentically.

Real estate investor, Eric Bowlin, holds the exact same belief. "Real estate is actually about people a lot more than the land," he says. "As a small company in real estate, i believe it is more info on branding yourself than branding the company. Make people want to work well with you."

Branding tip 3: Creatively create your own space

If, however, you take pride in having the creative chops to brand a thing that sticks out since it's new and innovative, you have a unique opportunity.

Cheryl Julcher of Yellow Brick Properties differentiated her brand from competitors by developing a brandname of homes called Zoetic Homes™. "Each home comes with a nutrition label, is *q*uality verified by an independent alternative party, and it is going to have a design that matches actual performance."

Branding tip 4: end up being the go-to expert

Being a specialist in your industry is yet another great way to set yourself apart. For Morgan Franklin, the secret ingredients were video and an energetic social media marketing presence.

"I have branded myself as a local expert and now have differentiated myself through the use of social networking, and more specifically, video," says Morgan. "I host a weekly real estate show this is certainly published to YouTube and Facebook. It has been huge since it has associated my brand with higher-end properties and even though We haven't had those listings."

Regarding the flipside, if you're young and inexperienced, you have of the same quality an opportunity to sell yourself. "Sell your inexperience (and youth if it applies to you) as a secured item," says agent Michelle Stansbury. "You would be hungry to succeed and are usually more likely to work harder to have homes sold as compared to agents who have already 'made it.' Inexperience isn't a total weakness and don't let anyone convince you it is."

Making it legal

One of the best aspects of engaging in real estate is the fact that for many states, there's really only 1 exam you'll want to pass. Study hard, and also you might possibly take action in a couple of months. Naturally, this differs slightly from state to mention, so be sure to check in with your state about regulations and rules.

In Florida, for example, you don't need to be an agent or a brokerage in order to open up a proper estate company. Based on Tim Frie, "You just need a broker-of-record that is an officer or manager regarding the company that is in charge of overseeing those things and transactions associated with the sales associates."

Of course, real estate qualifications aside, there are several things that you can do pretty early on, including finding out a name for the business, registering said name, applying for a Federal Tax ID, and obtaining any necessary business licenses and permits.

Choosing a business name is a strategic action. Plenty of notable real estate companies are named similar to this: Coldwell Banker, Keller William, Engel & Volkers, Long, and Foster. Not only did you want to emulate what was already proven on the market, but through the way that we offer service, we wanted something very deep to leave behind as a legacy which was due to our time and effort and dedication."

A great many other real estate agents also simply opt for their particular name, because it's a great way to attach your online business to your private brand.

Providing you know very well what things you ought to get done to start, the entire process of actually starting out is not all that hard. "Create a corporation, register your DBA, be sure you are in good standing with all boards and commissions," says Brad Pauly owner of Pauly Presley Realty, listing some key things you need to do to begin with. He also advises aspiring entrepreneurs to appear into getting liability insurance. That's key!

If you're still worried about how to start and how to really make it "legal," real estate broker James Brooks advises consulting a legal professional who focuses primarily on real estate law.

Getting financed

One of many great things about getting started in the real estate industry is that having plenty of cash on hand isn't always necessary.

It's also a company you could start part-time while you're still holding down a day job (though of course, you may need a flexible employer so you duck aside to occasionally take phone calls).

Joshua Jarvis, the master of Jarvis Team Realty, says, "The startup cost to launch in real estate is extremely low. I used the savings I experienced as well as for lower than $1,000 I happened to be in a position to start. Now my monthly budget is 10 times this, you don't actually need any money to start—or so most think."

The real thing to give some thought to, according to Joshua, is cash flow. "Don't just calculate the startup cost, calculate 'carrying cost,'" he says. "As in, exactly how many months it takes you to definitely start cash flowing. In real estate, you will find an excellent 60 days or even more before you might get paid."

For Hollywood real estate professional, Gwen Banta, having the finances to use the job seriously had a great deal to do with other revenue streams in the first place, including her act as an actress and writer.

When you do realize that you want investor funding or

a bank loan, writing a company plan is a good first step.

Real estate professional Jamal Asskoumi, took the finances for his business from personal savings. "If you can't fund the project yourself, ensure you discover how and how to locate investors," he says. "Also, create a flawless business plan to present in their mind."

If you're wondering what a proper estate business strategy looks like, take a good look at a few of our free trial realtor industry plans. They'll offer you a good idea of simple tips to structure your personal plan.

Setting up shop

For many people getting started in real estate, an office location is not necessary. As of this beginning phase, the focus is actually more about building a reputation in your chosen niche.

Real estate investor Eric Bowlin says, "The vast majority of people I know who work with real estate have started in their own home. It's more important to choose a target market rather than bother about a place for your storefront. At startup, you have to be flexible and in a position to rapidly adjust your plan if it's no longer working. A physical location will tie you down seriously to that market and make you less flexible while simultaneously adding expenses."

Of course, there may come an occasion once you do would you like to find a business location, hire employees, and get set up because of the right technology. Then again, hiring employees isn't for all. Eric says, "I've had employees in the past and I will not hire an employee again. The government regulations for employees is way too burdensome and expensive. Instead, everyone I work with is treated like a contractor and given a 1099."

In terms of technology, great customer relationship management software and a shared inbox solution is apparently the true estate agent's prized possession. Cheryl Julcher doesn't mince her words: "Our essential technology is our CRM, while the capability to work from anywhere 24/7."

And she's not the only one who advises using an instrument that helps you manage your contacts. For owner Joshua Jarvis, a beneficial CRM is practically indispensable, and it's something many real estate agents overlook. "The only real little bit of technology that might not be wise practice is a database. Whether it's an advanced CRM or simply Outlook, this can be huge. Your database is the business."

If you haven't been already convinced, doing well in real estate boils down to those personal connections you create, whether or perhaps not you've got a real-life office location. When you do hire employees, make certain they're a good fit along with your values as well as your brand first. All things considered, you don't wish to damage the truly amazing reputation you've spent a great deal time building.

Marketing and launching

Ask any real estate professional how they market their business, and you'll realize that "SEO" and "a good web presence" are common responses. Beyond the necessary networking you'll need to do, maintaining an online business in your real estate niche is key to your success.

Again, we get back to the importance of your own personal relationships with people. Getting business is all about seeing people, wherever these are typically, though it is equally important to possess an online presence to make certain that people can find you themselves!

Tim Frie says, "A large amount of real estate marketing is dependent on forming relationships, and you can do this most efficiently by blending an on-line strategy with a normal outreach and connection strategy."

If you don't have any customers, a great place to begin would be to reach out to people in your existing network. "Tell them in what you're doing," Tim says. "Ask when they know anyone who you are able to provide value to. If you're new and starting out, you need to put yourself in situations that enable you to definitely create new connections, meet new people, and supply value just by being yourself. Once people like you, they'll correlate your name with 'real estate' when they themselves or someone they know want to purchase or sell a house."

CAREER IN REAL ESTATE

A lifetime career in real estate can be both rewarding and challenging. Many people earn six-figure salaries, others, just a couple of thousand each year. Although it may be a good career: challenging, flexible and exciting, it's not for all. Here's what you need to know before you receive started in real estate.

Employed by Yourself

As a realtor, you're essentially doing work for yourself. Though there might be a few jobs available that pay an hourly rate, a normal real estate agent works strictly on commissions generated through the sale or rental of a residential or commercial property. In the same way you would before starting any business, you should make sure you've got the right character traits to operate on your own before becoming a real estate agent. You need to be:
- Ambitious
- Organized
- Dedicated
- Persevering
- Friendly
- Goal-oriented

A lifetime career in real estate ensures that you'll set your own personal schedule, but you'll need certainly to be organized and ambitious adequate to actually work at your organization every single day. Organization skills are important because you'll be dealing with contract deadlines, client appointments and follow-ups along with other professionals on the go. I asked Rhonda Taylor, a Realtor with Blakemore Real Estate, in Salt Lake City, Utah, for a few advice about starting out in the commercial. She told me:

Rhonda Taylor, Realtor"It's so great because you are your very own boss. You're able to dictate everything about your work day: You get to wake up when you wish, work when you need, work with who you need. The down side to this to that is you have to be really diligent and hold yourself accountable as it can be an easy task to not work when you don't have a boss looking over your shoulder. It's basically owning your own business. You're not planning to make money in the event that you don't work."

Most real estate agents don't make huge commissions throughout their first year. It requires time to build a client base and get familiar with how the business works. If you are going in thinking that it is something you'll try out for a few months, then throw in the towel if you aren't earning some huge cash, real estate may possibly not be for your needs. Before you will get started as an agent, you should ideally have six months to 1 year's worth of living expenses in the bank, which supplies a cushion whilst you build your business.

You'll need certainly to like working closely with people, because real estate sales is focused on helping people buy or sell their homes, so you'll be in frequent experience of clients every day. When asked about working with people, Rhonda said:

"You should be comfortable dealing with people. You have to have a client service mindset and start to become willing to help them when they need you. Whether you're helping a young couple find their first home, or representing a family who is selling their home and relocating, you should be confident, knowledgeable and most importantly, absolutely willing to go the additional mile for individuals."

Finding a brokerage

As a uni**q**ue agent, you'll work under a genuine estate broker. Brokers have typically been in the business for many years and also have additional training, knowledge and an independent license. They are needed to carry insurance that protects buying and selling clients, in addition to real estate professionals. Brokers oversee agents and review purchase contracts for errors. In the event that you make an error during a transaction plus the case goes to court, your broker's insurance covers legal fees and settlement costs. In short, the broker is ultimately the responsible party in a transaction. In substitution for carrying this responsibility, your broker will re**q**uire a portion of one's sales commissions and may charge you other fees.

Choosing the best broker is essential for career success. The best broker for you might vary, depending on your previous knowledge, dependence on mentoring and financial expectations. Some brokers are extremely hands-on and provide formal training during your first 12 months in the commercial. Others simply provide insurance and a recognizable brand, but don't expect to spend much time to you.

It's a smart idea to visit several brokers before you get started in your real estate career. By taking a look at what each is offering, you could make the right decision for you personally.

The "Split"

The broker carries the duty for each and every transaction, and spends money on insurance. He also provides a workplace, branding and often marketing. Large national brokerages, such as for example Coldwell Banker or Century 21, advertise on tv, radio plus in print ads. Each local brokerage must pay franchise fees to pay for that marketing. Smaller, local brokerages may not advertise nationally, nevertheless they work tirelessly to create a recognizable brand and often advertise in local publications, on local billboards and by participating in local events. The broker must cover his costs, so he takes a portion of every commission that a realtor earns. This can be called a "split."

When you initially start out in the industry, your portion of the split will undoubtedly be low. You might start off with a 70/30 split, or even as little as 60/40 (you obtain the larger for the two amounts). Needless to say, your broker will be so much more hands-on in the beginning, providing additional training, mentoring and advice.

As you become more experienced and successful, your split goes up. Most brokers have a method put up where, as you reach a certain dollar quantity of sales, you are going into the next level. Standard splits for successful agents are around 80/20 and certainly will be up to 90/10.

How Much Cash Can You Make?

Most real estate professionals are paid completely on commission. In residential real estate transactions, your home seller typically pays around 6% for the sales price towards the agent(s) who handle the sale (Commission rates vary slightly, but 6% is common). The two agents split the commission, then that amount is split because of the broker. Here's an example:

Joe lists Sally's house for $100,000. Mike brings his clients to see the home and his clients end up buying it. Following the transaction closes, Joe receives $3,000 and thus does Mike. Both Joe and Mike work on an 80/20 split with regards to brokers. So, each receive a commission look for $2400. They'll be responsible for paying income taxes on that amount.

How much money you'll make is based on two factors:

1) The housing marketplace, including the availability of virginia homes and the availability of mortgage loans for prospective buyers.

2) Your ambition. The more you work, the more

money you'll make.

"There are countless possibilities. Your earnings isn't limited. It depends as to how hard you intend to work and what you want to put into it. Just how many jobs exist where you are able to earn a six-figure income without a college degree? That doesn't mean that you don't need an education, though. You'll have to set up lots of time learning about the business, about the real estate market and about techniques like marketing and networking. It's an education… just not on a college campus!"

What you ought to Get Going

Getting into a real estate career is relatively inexpensive, when compared with other businesses. Here's what you'll have to start:

Real Estate License

Though reQuirements vary from state-to-state, all reQuire licensing. Consult your local Board of Realtors or your state's Department of Real Estate to learn what you need to do to obtain a license. Typically, you'll be expected to go to training classes. Then you'll take a situation exam. Once you've passed, you'll pay a fee and receive a license. Most states reQuire also continuing education and license renewal.

MLS Access

The MLS (Multiple Listing Service), is a comprehensive online tool that allows agents to find properties for purchasing clients, and list properties for selling clients. The MLS charges a monthly fee for access.

Board of Realtor Dues

If you opt to join the Board of Realtors, you'll pay annual dues. Though it is not mandatory that you join, most real estate professionals do. Look at the National Association of Realtors site for more information on the benefits of becoming a Realtor®.

Computer

Ideally, a laptop that you could take to you towards the office also to client meetings.

Smart Phone

You'll be from the phone a lot as a realtor, taking calls from clients, getting updates from appraisers, home inspectors and loan officers, and setting appointments with potential new clients. Get a model with GPS so that you can easily find addresses when taking buyer clients to look at homes. You'll also be able to remain in contact via email and text, and that can look up properties when you look at the MLS (Multiple Listing Service).

Car

While you don't need a fancy car, it should be in reasonable working condition. Ensure that is stays neat and clutter-free; you'll drive clients around occasionally.

Business Cards

While many people don't make use of these any more, they're still a staple for real estate agents.

Signage

You'll need signs to market homes for sale, open houses and other events. Design your own signs utilizing your broker's logo (generally in most states this really is required). Consult your state's Real Estate Division for any other items to include on your own sign that may be required by law.

Spend money on a variety of signage: directional signs to help people find your listings, vinyl banners for larger-format advertising and car magnets to alert people that you are a realtor. Some signs can be made to work with every property (such as for instance directional signage). Others must certanly be designed especially for one listing (list the features, price and address of a home, by way of example).

Clothing

Dressing professionally is essential when you look at the realtor industry. Spend money on some nice suits, quality shoes and accessories in order for you'll look nice and feel confident.

Get Going

If you were to think that a vocation in real estate is a good fit for you personally, get going! Are you when you look at the real estate industry?

REAL ESTATE COMMISSION RATES

Real estate commissions are one of the more debated factors in selling a house. So, should home sellers be paying commissions after all? What's really reasonable? How can homeowners get the best mixture of value and net proceeds?

- •Real Estate Commissions Because Of The Numbers
- •89% of home sellers are employing real estate professionals
- •The typical rate of commission is 6% of this closing price
- •Luxury real estate specialists often charge 10%
- •The standard commission on rentals is 10% for the lease

Where Does the Money Go?

Some genuinely believe that Realtor rates are costly. The information shows that the typical agent barely makes minimum wage. So, where does the cash go?

Buyer & Seller Agent Splits

The gross commission is typically split 50/50 between the agents who represent the buyer and seller. So, out of a gross 6% commission, your agent would only typically get 3% gross.

Brokerage Splits

Out of that 3% the agent needs to split with their office. This generally ranges from a 50/50 to as high as a 90/10 split. So, on average the actual agent may only get 1.5% of that 6% commission.

Agent Costs

Then the agent has to cover their costs. That means office fees, technology fees, license fees, marketing, and insurance fees. Then there are the specific costs they need to spend money on for your house. They've been betting this cash on their capability to market your house, and they're doing it out of their own pocket upfront. Between transportation, signs, open houses, printing flyers, newspaper and magazine ads, photography, and internet marketing, this will probably easily be thousands of dollars. That is just the tip regarding the iceberg of what great agents will do as well.

On a $100,000 home sale, at a 6% gross commission rate, the agent may only get $1,500 BEFORE a few of these costs come out. That doesn't include income taxes either. Most might turn out to be out of pocket on a transaction such as this. Which may be different on a $1M home, however the expenses do rise because of the level of a home being marketed on the market too. Consider that a single page ad on a top-level website or newspaper can very quickly run $5,000 to $7,000 alone.

Being fair; in fact most agents are probably vastly underpaid. That's one of many reasons that 90% of the latest agents go broke within their first year.

In the event that you just make an effort to sell yourself; which means investing in every associated with the marketing yourself, and spending money on it upfront.

Plus, you'll definitely need an actual estate attorney to greatly help negotiate, complete contracts, and accompany you at the closing. Once you start marketing you'll also realize that you might be mostly approached by Realtors, plus they aren't going to show your property with their interested and *q*ualified buyers unless you agree to pay a commission.

Then you will find FSBO websites or flat fee MLS services that may list your home on their sites, or sell you DIY marketing materials. Again, this really is an upfront investment, with no guarantee of results. Whatever they don't typically tell you is that no one will probably show your premises, until you offer commission to buyers' agents. Like it or not, many agents will curate the menu of homes they show their customers on the basis of the commission offered. So, to make this work, expect to offer 3%. The downside is you continue to have no representation, or qualified advice, but your buyer does. For in-depth breakdown of additional reasons as to why, visit our article 11 main reasons why FSBO Sellers Should Reconsider Hiring an agent.

Note, that the master of one of the largest FSBO services ironically used an agent for the sale of his very own home.

It's Exactly About the Web

All sorts of things that it's exactly about the net. A part of this is basically the net proceeds. If just how much you are going to place in your pocket on closing day is exactly what is most significant, it doesn't matter if an agent charges 1% or 10%. It is about this net number. Some agents just have more established networks and so are better sales people. They could negotiate higher sales prices.

Then there is also the internet value. Your net proceeds are a part of this. So, is how *q*uickly you sell, and just how the ability is. Every day you wait to market costs money. If an individual agent charges a little more but sells your house 2 months faster, they may be the most effective deal. Then sellers should take into account how professional the agent is supposed to be, and how seamless they can make the process.

Commission Rates Are Negotiable

Everything is negotiable in real estate therefore we have tactics to how to go about achieving this within our article just how to Negotiate Commission Rates with Real Estate Agents. Don't discount using an agent as you think you must pay 6% to 10% in commissions. Agents may negotiate lower rates with regards to the variety of transaction, the services required, and frequency of business.

For example; if you should be an actual estate investor buying and selling 10 homes four weeks, a real estate agent may be willing to work a 50% off deal in return for the quantity. If they're receiving a referral from a reliable source they could offer a modest discount, while still giving a full-service experience. If you don't require the agent to host open houses, and so they can secure a buyer directly, without the need to split with another agent, chances are they may offer a price reduction relative to their savings.

Bonuses & Incentives

Home sellers might also work with their agents on bonuses and incentives. These could be paid by the seller, or out from the listing agent's commission. As an example; offering a $10,000 bonus for a complete price offer which closes within 1 month, or contributing 3% of the purchase price toward buyer's closing costs.

Real estate commission rates

In accordance with the National Association of Realtors 87% of home buyers come through an agent. Between this fact, while the net numbers and value provided by good agents, even standard commission rates could possibly be cheap. Still, there clearly was room to negotiate, and thousands of dollars may be saved by getting top agents to compete through the UpNest.com platform.

IS CAREER AS A REAL ESTATE AGENT RIGHT FOR YOU

A lot of people think that a real estate career is simple money, and it will be usually before long. And there's much more to it than that.

You don't need to be a "salesperson" which will make a good residing in this field. Real estate is primarily a site business, so serving your customers well contributes to your success. But the majority of people have found real estate to be an all natural transition from another sales career plus they believe that it really is more fulfilling. After all, you are helping people with what exactly is often one of several largest financial transactions they're going to make inside their lives.

Needless to say, every career has drawbacks. It is a matter of balancing the great from the bad and gauging your tolerance for the bad. You are your own boss as a real estate agent, but this comes with a great deal of added responsibility and a little bit of a cash investment to begin with.

Education Requirements Can Be Minimal

Its not necessary a college degree to be a real estate agent, although education is normally helpful in any career you pursue. States almost universally require which you have at the least a higher school diploma or GED, and you needs to be at least 18 yrs old. Some states have training requirements and you will need certainly to pass a licensing exam, but you can repeat this in significantly less time than it will require to make a bachelor's degree.

Starting out, you'll almost certainly need certainly to complete a pre-licensing course, nevertheless the investment of time could be minimal, as little as 30 days from start to finish. The exam itself can be challenging in a few states. It's often divided in to a state-level section with a second part aimed at national laws and issues, and you will need certainly to pass both.

The National Association of Realtors regularly sponsors courses as you are able to enroll in to prepare yourself, and they're going to look great on the resume, too.

The Cash Is Great, Eventually

You're typically stuck with similar wage or salary week in and week out once you work the standard job, unless and until your employer chooses to be magnanimous and offer you a raise. Any limits to your eventual earnings are the ones you add in position yourself if you are a real estate agent. Exactly how much you get is commonly directly proportional to exactly how much and just how hard you work.

Having said that, the word "eventual" is key here. You won't reap a windfall very first week face to face. It simply does not happen by doing this, and you should be ready to deal with that. It can come down seriously to your temperament and your tolerance for just a little financial stress.

You'll have to spend some money to get started. There is the licensing exam and any training you will need to start. You will also need business cards, an advertising budget, and a good, reliable car. And you will have all your very own bills to cover as well.

Some experts' advise that it could 6 months to a year before you receive very first commission check because commissions are usually paid at the conclusion of transactions. You will need to put in a fair little bit of work to arrive at that time, and you will need ample savings to survive through that time.

Real estate professionals earn a median salary of approximately $47,880 at the time of 2017, in line with the Bureau of Labor Statistics. Median implies that 1 / 2 of all agents make a lot more than this and half earn less. And also this encompasses people who regularly deal in seven-figure properties along with agents who dabble in the field part-time. The two extremes tend to balance out the numbers.

You'll Enjoy Flexible Hours, Sometimes

This perk comes with a caveat, too, also it comes down to what's vital that you you. Nobody will probably require that you punch an occasion clock at 9 a.m. and stay planted at your desk until 5 p.m., Monday through Friday. You are able to set your personal hours, and you can move them around to support your personal needs. If you like to grab your youngster from school, you are able to do that.

The flip side is the fact that nearly all your real estate clients is supposed to be punching time clocks or will likely to be otherwise confined to create working schedules. You will need to make your self available if they are if you wish to do a great business. This often means working nights, weekends, as well as some holidays.

You're Helping People

The helping facet of real estate work is a big advantage for altruistic types. Your clients are on the verge of taking what might be the most important financial step up their lives, perhaps buying their first home or selling their long-time family home to downsize since they're retiring. In any case, you may expect nerves and often buyers' or sellers' remorse.

You do not need a Ph.D. in psychology to manage all of this, but having plenty of compassion and patience can really help, especially if you prefer giving freely of both.

The Tech Advantage

Technology advances and also the mobile world will help agents that aren't exceptionally people-oriented to be successful in real estate. When you can work a great website that's mobile device-friendly, if you can handle some social website posting, and in case you respond quickly to emails or text messages, you should have a genuine opportunity to relate genuinely to prospects.

The professionals of a Real Estate Career

You'll probably find very diverse cause of choosing an actual estate career if you question a team of brand-new agents. Many love the helping nature of this job, although some desire to exercise their independent nature and start to become their own bosses. But it takes commitment and a good investment of effort, time, and money to create an effective real estate career.

You'll get a whole lot in return. You are an unbiased contractor, so you can control your own business. Your earnings isn't limited. It is predicated on your talent and your work ethic. It is possible to build future business with great service and client referrals.

The Cons of a vocation in Real Estate

If you're an unbiased contractor, you're on your own with regards to making certain your business thrives. Income could be quite a while in coming when you first start off. The first months and years in real estate could be feast or famine before you get going.

There is a top failure rate for new agents. Liability and risk are part of representing clients. You'll need insurance because some mistakes, such as for example neglecting to disclose a material fact about the property or neglecting inspections, will get you sued.

Pros:

•You're an Independent Contractor and control your own business.

•Your income is not limited & based on your skills and work ethic.

•Set your personal working arrangements and vacations.

•Work outdoors as well as in varied locations.

•Build future business with great service and client referrals.

•Enjoy helping people in another of their largest financial transactions.

Cons:

•You're an Independent Contractor as well as on your own to understand the business.

•Income can be a long time getting going and "feast or famine".

•You need to be available if the clients would like you.

•There's a top failure rate for new agents.

Liability and risk are part of representing clients.

REAL ESTATE CAREERS FOR THOSE WHO DON'T WANT TO BUY AND SELL HOMES

Whenever you think of a proper estate professional, you likely get an extremely specific image of a residential real estate professional, helping people purchase and sell their homes and performing all of the related tasks. This is certainly definitely the best-known real estate career, however it's not the only person.

If you can find components of a residential real estate sales career that are appealing to you and others which are not, perchance you will be better designed for an alternative career path in real estate. Lets explore some of the lesser-known real estate careers available and help you discover one that is the best fit for your needs.

Commercial Real Estate Salesperson

Commercial real estate professionals help clients lease, buy, and sell commercial property. There are lots of similarities between commercial and residential agents, but there are several unique differences as well. For one, the commercial real estate sales process often takes more than the residential process. And also the needs and concerns associated with clients you certainly will serve are not the same.

Both residential and commercial real estate careers require that you earn your real estate salesperson's license. Legally, there isn't any post-secondary education necessary to become a commercial real estate agent in most states. However, most commercial brokerages expect their candidates to at the least have a bachelor's degree. Like a residential agent, commercial agents must "hang their license" with (work beneath) an agent. You can find out about the commercial real estate career path in this essay.

Real Estate Broker

An actual estate broker owns and runs a proper estate brokerage company. To become a broker, you must earn an enhanced license. Every state's rules are very different, but must require that you log a prescribed length of time as an authorized agent before you can earn a broker's license. Real estate brokers operate independently, which means that they keep 100% of these commission split. They often times likewise have real estate professionals working under them inside their office, who they hire, support, and manage. There was a substantial number of responsibility that comes with running a brokerage. As a result, some brokers choose not to represent clients within the sale or purchase of real estate and dedicate most of their energy to running an effective brokerage.

Business Broker

Business brokers aid and assist buyers and sellers within the purchase of businesses. At first, this may seem like the exact same job as a commercial real estate professional, however it's not. For example, commercial agents could be in charge of selling a dental office. But a company broker would sell the business that occupies that office along with the property. Some states require a license to become a small business broker. Even if you live in a state that will not require one, it is recommended that real estate professionals complete specialized business broker training to achieve success at it.

Loan Officer

Loan officers play a critical role in the real estate transaction process, since most buyers will demand that loan which will make a proper estate purchase. There are loan officers who focus on both mortgage (residential) and commercial lending. They work for lending institutions, like banks, and work as an intermediary amongst the consumer plus the lending institution. They work to comprehend their clients' needs and supply lending solutions tailored to your individual or company they're serving. When an ideal option is identified, in addition they assist individuals in the application for the loan process.

Home Inspector

It is incredibly rare today for a house to sell without a home inspection. Home inspectors examine, analyze, and report regarding the physical condition of a residential property. They play a crucial role in presenting most of the details about the home, therefore the buyers can make a decision about whether or not to go forward making use of their planned purchase. Home inspection professionals often (not always) begin their career in another of the building trades. When they actually choose to be a house inspector, they typically complete education to learn more about home systems these are generally not really ac**q**uainted with therefore the particulars of running a house inspection business. Some states re**q**uire home inspectors to complete education and be licensed, while other states try not to.

Real Estate Appraiser

Real estate appraisers provide an estimate of land and building value before real estate is sold, developed, mortgaged, taxed, or insured. Because there are so many factors that influence the value of property, including specific local market conditions, real estate appraisers typically practice in an exceedingly specific and defined geographic location. Real estate appraisers are re**q**uired to complete specific education and meet licensure re**q**uirements to practice within their profession.

Real Estate Assistant

Real estate assistants make use of agents and brokers to serve clients and manage the day-to-day tasks associated with helping them buy and sell real estate. The amount of service an assistant can offer without a license varies from state to state. That is why, some agents and brokers prefer to hire assistants that have earned their license. Real estate practitioners vary in how they pay their real estate assistants. Some pay a predictable hourly wage or salary. Others offer a commission split.

Real Estate Developer

Real estate development is a career field that requires the vision to consider a blank canvas of land and imagine what it could be. Many tasks fall under the umbrella of real estate development, & most developers do a little mixture of them. Developers purchase land, finance deals, and manage the growth plan for a given bit of real estate from just starting to end. Real estate development is normally a high-risk, high-reward career. Developers shoulder all the front-end investment, but ultimately maximize the worthiness associated with the land prior to taking that space to advertise. If they've done their homework and demand can there be when it comes to specific property they've developed, there's an important financial opportunity waiting for them in the back end.

House Flipper

Reality television has made the phrase "flipping a house" something all of us understand. If you're just the right person for this type of work, it may be *q*uite lucrative. However, as we've also learned from reality television, the number of individuals who are actually good at flipping houses is significantly smaller than how many individuals who think they're good at it. House flippers typically purchase a house centered on potential. They invest in improving the property through their particular (or hired) labor and ultimately try to resell the home for a profit.

Landlord or Property Manager

Landlords own property they rent to tenants. That property can consist of land, commercial buildings, apartments, and houses. Property managers work on behalf of a landlord to perform many different services that will include marketing rentals, maintenance and upkeep, rent collection, giving an answer to tenant concerns, and also handling evictions. While many landlords hire property managers or property management companies, additionally, it is not unusual for a landlord to behave because their own property manager.

HOW TO FINANCE YOUR REAL ESTATE BUSINESS

Hard Money Lender

Hard money lenders are a financing tactic often employed by real estate investors. Instead of coming from a bank, the funds for those investments originate from a personal individual or group. Because these loans do not need to go through any corporate procedures, they frequently have looser *q*ualifying re*q*uirements and may be secured faster. Additionally, private lenders may be much more available to backing risky projects.

Knowing that, investors should always be confident within their ability to pay back the loan *q*uickly before signing regarding the dotted line. Hard money loans often have very high rates of interest and require a big down payment or personal collateral. They likewise have much shorter terms than traditional loans, averaging only per year or two.

Microloans

Microloans are generally geared toward newer businesses or startups that need capital to come up with further growth. Whilst the name suggests, these loans are smaller than what's usually offered with traditional bank financing. Lower balances mean that microloan programs are less limiting in terms of their qualifying requirements like credit rating, which is often a comfort to those concerned with borrowing above their means.

However, microloans may possibly not be a great fit for all. Though these loans can go up to $50,000, the common loan is only about $13,000, therefore it's crucial that you gauge overhead costs accordingly. Also, their attention rates are typically greater than those offered through standard loan programs.

Real Estate Crowdfunding

In the past, investing in real estate was restricted to individuals with deep pockets, but because the passage of the 2012 JOBS Act, crowdfunding has grown to become an easy method for investors to diversify their portfolios at a far lower cost. In place of being forced to search out and restore properties by themselves, investors can browse crowdfunding platforms to select from a listing of available investment projects for which to participate. They then are able to finance shares of the property at the lowest cost sometimes as little as $1,000 and collect a percentage regarding the profits or rent payments when the project has been completed.

Having said that, this kind of investing does come with elevated risk. Investors have significantly less control of the outcome than they might in a traditional fix-and-flip scenario. Be aware that there could be a longer wait for profits on return, depending on how each deal is structured. Additionally, understand that if the project fails, it is the investors that will shoulder the loss as opposed to the builder. You are able to find out more about crowdfunding in this in-depth article.

SBA Loans

SBA loans are so-named as the Small Business Association offers a warranty of repayment to banks which can be willing to underwrite loans for new entrepreneurs. The guarantee lets banks become more willing to take risks. As the affordability of a loan depends on an investor's unique situation, generally these loans have higher borrowing limits up to $2,000,000. SBA loans also come with longer terms, lower down payments, and protection against balloon payments, which will help businesses maintain a reliable cash flow.

It's important to see SBA loans can't be used to spend money on real estate but can be employed to start an actual estate business, such as a brokerage or property management fund. Unfortunately, the security that SBA loans offer comes at a cost. Not only is it at the mercy of high fees, investors should have a top credit score and also show significant profit to their tax returns in order to qualify. The applying process can also be lengthy and requires the borrower to put on personal assets as collateral.

ROBS

If applying for that loan just isn't for you personally, a rollover as business startup (ROBS) provider may be the best choice. This method of financing allows small business owners to attract funds from existing retirement accounts without incurring tax or withdrawal penalties. Considering that the cash is their particular, there aren't any debt payments, leaving them absolve to invest the total amount into business growth. Also, in the event that the business enterprise should fail, this leaves no negative effect on their credit rating or any other assets.

Before committing to a ROBS strategy, an investor needs to be certain to weigh the risks. Regarding the one hand, they may be able only draw the money inside their existing accounts, which means their available funds can be smaller than they might be with a loan. Consistent with that, if the investor chooses to invest the entirety of their retirement funds to the business, therefore the business fails, they may be left without security in retirement. Just like SBA loans, ROBS is not used to purchase real estate.

REAL ESTATE AND ARTIFICIAL INTELLIGENCE

"An Artificial Intelligence (AI) may be the science & designing of creating intelligent machines, mainly intelligent PC programs" – in accordance with the father of Artificial Intelligence John McCarthy. This is the solution to making software or a computer robot that will think intelligently like a person. It will be the notion of having machines that may feel like a human.

Nowadays artificial intelligence is changing the world in lot of ways. It is about making our lives better yet than before. There are lots of companies are receiving success considerably by way of artificial intelligence. One of many growing companies is real estate.

Today AI is not taking the host to real estate agents. The technology like AI helps them to truly save time & money as well. We're going to discuss the benefits of real estate and artificial intelligence.

Artificial intelligence will alter the real estate industry

Nowadays there is absolutely no doubt that artificial intelligence will alter all in the real estate. Let's see how artificial intelligence will alter the true estate industry

Data Management

Many realtors manage huge amounts of information. The total of data is increasing from year to year. In the event that human realtors do this entire work by hand – it takes sufficient time to manage it. Into the real estate professionals fre*q*uently re*q*uires the data in regards to the property. You can automate data collection & data management through artificial intelligence (AI).

Getting Data-Driven Insights

Artificial intelligence (AI) receives the exact same patterns when you look at the data, although that data is not yet determined. Even experience realtors sometimes are helpless to recognize complex patterns. Another issue isn't just to find the data but in addition to obtain insights as a result. Artificial intelligence person finds the specific area is most likely to explode in popularity in later.

Property Price Calculations

There's a challenge when you look at the real estate sector: it really is quite difficult to calculate the worth of this property. Generally, the true estate agents find out the cost according to the former sales costs without taking into consideration many points.

These points are including neighborhoods, environment changes, improvements, infrastructure, and transportation and so on. Every one of these features influence the finish property value. Artificial Intelligence can resolve that problem with pattern identification by exposing the points that impact the property cost.

Lead Management

Lead management was the center of every company & business into the Real Estate is not the particular case. Artificial Intelligence or AI may process plenty of data when you look at the search for vital information. Realtors and other marketing agency use that data in marketing functions like advertising, post-sales, pre-sales an such like. That data assists the real estate agents to obtain the property clients most likely to buy.

Customers Interaction

Nowadays people face the latest, unsighted before, chatbots that use natural language processing and artificial intelligence. That chatbots work quickly and smartly to process complicated user **q**ueries. That chatbots are self-learned. Chatbots can learn into the way of human communication.

Reduces the cost of real estate services

You are able to save switch office from offline to online offices by making use of artificial intelligence improvement technologies. Thus realtors can reduce their office costs as well as in return provide their services to clients at a low cost.

Helps in the commercial transaction

Artificial intelligence (AI) can be used in the bank in order to make business deal faster & safer. Also, it can stop cheating by verifying bank accounts & notifying you will find any issues.

How will artificial intelligence in real estate work

Two phrases: Lease Abstraction.

Lease abstraction a method of collecting from a rental agreement for desire to analysis & modeling. Nevertheless, LEVERTON develops the technique with artificial intelligence. Leases are specially made the actual estate sector engaging.

Leases are complicated, and lengthy deeds are generally consisting of a sizable page of data, and examining them may take anywhere from 4 – 8 hours.

Leases could be dropped and pulled into a platform with LEVERTON's artificial intelligence. This may examine those leases and in line with the information you give and that can mechanically pull the data & show them in a talented manner.

These kinds of analytics in real estate save time, lessen the total expense basis, and lastly, give a more well-aimed procedure for lease abstraction.

The true estate sector doesn't have significant

technological advancement. Nevertheless the MRI Software brings the way to keep its customers contemporary with great & flexible solutions. Also it helps companies to succeed in the present day time.

LEVERTON is functioning to obtain the new technology to your market by implementing an artificial intelligence that boosts the method of lease abstraction.

Whilst the artificial intelligence of LEVERTON is a time-saving machine, perhaps one of the most valuable & unique attributes of its service is its ability to draw a complete of data from leases & agreements.

This data will give you your company an even more comprehensive snapshot of that rental agreement. It will qualify you to definitely make successful business resolution concerning your property.

The true estate field can just do it utilizing the modern time. And yes it is preparing to meet with the challenges of today using this technological advancement.

What does the industry think?

In accordance with the research among real estate experts on the basis of the current utilization of AI, its future use and what points might stop its acceptance, there are some important aspects about artificial intelligence and realtor industry. These factors will give a clear conception concerning the aftereffect of artificial intelligence throughout the real estate business. They are including:

• There is only one person in five (18%) comment that artificial intelligence will substitute human efficiency in the long run

• More than half (54%) regarding the real estate experts already use artificial intelligence to promote the keyword search system in the realtor industry deal.

• Almost two-thirds of people (69%) trust artificial intelligence provides their company a competitive benefit by qualifying a higher amount and lots of data to be searched at high speed.

• Over fifty-three percent recover too little dependence in artificial intelligence's ability to match human knowledge

& decision-making

When asked where AI gets the best influence regarding progressing the competency of processes, over three-quarters of consumer says identifying related data in an important data room. Also, two-thirds of individuals say it really is eliminating time-consuming manual review system.

However, it doesn't mean the battle of technology vs. humans. Irrespective of it is to automate a huge wide range of methods, artificial intelligence (AI) will continue to work best in combination with human efficiency & intelligence.

Artificial intelligence needs to learn from human attitude & there isn't any substitute for years of expertise, knowledge, and inspiration. Nevertheless, artificial intelligence (AI) goes with those aspects and adds massive worth by simply making real estate processes far more efficient, automated and cost-effective.

REAL ESTATE MARKETING

Real estate marketing is focused on promoting your brand as a real estate agent and securing buyer and seller leads by sharing your listings on social media, advertising your agency, and building your internet site content. For fresh marketing ideas, take a look at our ultimate range of marketing advice from top-producing agents below.

Market Yourself

The National Association of Realtors (NAR) states that 90% of home buyers house hunt online. While the largest real estate website with more than 160 million visitors per month, Zillow could be the first place you have to be. Zillow Premier Agent is Zillow's platform that lets you advertise on local Zillow and Trulia listings. We estimate that for almost any $1 you may spend, you'll earn $2.60 in commissions. Follow this link to get rates in your town.

Offer Home Valuations to fully capture Seller Leads

The most difficult marketing challenges for real estate agents is capturing seller leads. Real Geeks offers a house valuation tool that you can put right on your site. By inputting a few details, sellers can create a valuation report for his or her property and receive monthly updates. You reap the benefits of collecting these seller email addresses, that are added to your selection of leads. View here for a home valuation tool demo.

Leverage Influencer Marketing

One good way to gain social validity and expand the reach and hype of an inventory is by using influencers and public relations. For example, if a list is unique, you can get in touch with local bloggers and Instagram influencers — whose followership matches your target buyer — and also have them create related content and share it with their followers. There are several websites and blogs which have an apartment of the week showcase that one can try and have your space featured in.

Generate Referrals by Hosting Community Events

My favorite marketing advice would be to embrace community engagement. As an example, in May and June, we host two free community paper shred events — one in Los Alamitos, California, while the other in Brea. The big event reduces paper within the landfill and helps people reduce identity theft. To help spread the phrase, our agents farm various neighborhoods with flyers and door hangers. People can shred up to five boxes of paper at no cost, which will be about a $100 savings.

Make Your Website Your Storefront

Our primary marketing tool is our website. In today's market, it will be the storefront to your company. Having a mobile-friendly site that ranks saturated in organic traffic will surpass all of your paid digital advertising. It not only has to showcase both you and your differentiators, but in addition has to portray attention to detail when promoting your listings. The photography needs to be on point, that you simply will use in every marketing piece, including social networking posts.

Create Real Estate Websites

One of the ways we can generate five or more new leads daily is by using our local community pages. The thing that makes this such a powerful marketing idea may be the fact you might be reverse-engineering focus on generate real estate leads. When you put the work in up front, these leads are continuous.

Provide a Complimentary Moving Truck

My n. 1 marketing idea for real estate is my complimentary moving truck, available for use by clients who buy or sell a home. I also provide the truck for use to nonprofit organizations. It's a moving billboard, and no other agent in the region offers a moving truck. It gets lots of attention.

In addition strategically park it in high-traffic areas when not being used. When events have been in town that focus on homeowners, including the home or boat show, my moving truck will likely to be there.

Use Instagram Stories

Instagram Stories are huge in 2019, given that the sheer number of daily active users of Instagram Stories has surpassed 500 million. The real question is how to use them to offer more homes and grow your local brand recognition. Engagement is absolutely key, so make use of the polls and Q&A stickers within Stories. Ask questions, use GIFs, and make the content as simple to interact with as possible.

The more people you build relationships with, the greater they will remember you, while the more you train the Instagram algorithm that you have great content, which IG will reward with an increase of organic reach than if no one ever engaged with you. You can run contests and giveaways within Instagram Stories. As an example, have people take screenshots of them listening to your podcast, ask them to direct message you the image, and then choose one at random to win something. Master how to get people engaged and coming back for more, and you'll win.

Send Postcards

To offer your postcards staying power, Wachtel recommends using "fridge-worthy" subjects like best metro area hikes, a good go-to recipe for guacamole, helpful tips from what NFL referee signals mean, or advice for timing your Thanksgiving meal perfectly. As she explains, "We regularly hear from clients as well as prospective agents who end up calling us or their agent directly based on a postcard that were hanging to their refrigerator or memo board for months on end."

Optimize Your Facebook Page

With millions of daily users, you'd be remiss not to ever utilize Facebook as a marketing tool these days. Download this free ebook from Matterport to learn about some of the biggest improvements you could make to your company Facebook page, how exactly to set up paid campaigns, and lots of other helpful tips. It also discusses how to convert these contributes to actual sales. Get started today.

Create Subdivision Website Pages

When you may not be able to compete with Zillow for search phrases like "houses on the market in [city]," you might be in a position to rank on Google for more niche search phrases for micro-neighborhoods, pretty streets, or subdivisions. Photos, videos, an industry snapshot, school district information, and pertinent information regarding a subdivision or area are great methods to build organic traffic to your website.

Highlight Homes With Professional Photography

95% of buyers start their search on the internet, plus the **q**uality for the photography should determine if a residential property gets seen or not. It's also a known truth that when the photographs are not excellent, the home buyers won't stop and read the description of the property. Even though a realtor suggests a residential property with their customer, the buyer with a busy schedule will decide based solely on the photos if they like to spend their time planning to visit a property. It's difficult to overcome the first bad reaction even though they do start to see the property.

Use Unique Décor to Set Your Listing Apart

Have one **q**uirky item in the house. Because of this, when buyers are referring to it, they could say, "the house with the giant Buddha" or "the orange rug house." Have a thing that stays inside their mind about the style or design. Sometimes, a perfectly nice, normal house can be forgotten about when it is the middle house of six houses seen through the same day.

Live Stream Your Agency's Day-to-Day

When scrolling through a social media marketing feed, a "Live Now" tag is more or less irresistibly clickable. Folks are naturally curious. Seeing an innovative new listing when it comes to first time? You will want to show your audience via live stream? They'll feel just like they're getting the inside scoop, and you'll be able to grow your audience to get more leads. That's a win-win situation.

In this edition of Beverly Hills superstar broker Peter Lorimer's amazing "Magic Minute" series, he walks you through the process.

Choose Words That Sell

If you're working as a listing agent, it's important to create descriptions which will jump from the page and grab the buyer. A beneficial tactic is always to appeal to the buyer's emotions. Use keywords that paint a photo. It's not only about sharing facts, but additionally about selling stories.

Market Leader enables you to buy actual buyer and seller leads who wish to be contacted by a realtor. This lets you create your stable of leads and target these with compelling listing descriptions. Check to see if Market Leader has leads available in your ZIP code.

Focus Your Marketing Efforts

We have discovered that marketing more often to an inferior geographic area works much better than marketing wide and shallow. We use a mixture of direct mail, calls, targeted search engine optimization (SEO), and pay-per-click (PPC) to find our customers.

Make Connections with Local Businesses

Real estate is a people business. To market yourself successfully also to attract new leads and clients, you first need certainly to make them like you as an individual also to demonstrate to them that you care about the area area and community. Establish relations with the local shopkeepers, business owners, and employees. Take part in local events. A few of these efforts will not only cause you to feel better and more engaged but may also cause you to be noticed off their agents and brokers who aren't so involved in the life of the neighborhood community.

Showcase Your Charitable Side

I believe the simplest way to achieve success at real estate will be supply the prospective customers something to consider you by. Real estate professionals have to differentiate themselves, additionally the solution to accomplish that is through Giveback Homes, which will be an organization of agents that builds homes for people in need. This organization is creating social change, giving real estate professionals a good social platform and ways to differentiate themselves from the competition.

Create a Blog That Answers Client Questions

Real estate is often a hot topic of discussion, so any talking points I'm able to provide in a blog is good reading. We have worked diligently over the past 38 years positioning myself as an industry expert in neuro-scientific luxury residential real estate sales in the Hamptons. Clients and customers desire to hear from me. Whether it is my update on current market conditions or my opinion/personal views on design and architecture. My breadth of business and market knowledge is encapsulated when you look at the data I provide with quotes from me often utilized in the press.

Create a Video Series to generally share With Leads

Social media is a vital option to both remain in touch with individuals you realize and also to ensure you get your name call at front of brand new people. We post regularly on Facebook, Instagram, Twitter, and so on. We do a weekly video series called "Ask the Realtor" we just finished season one and generally are planning season two and turn those short videos into Facebook ads. The videos typically earn around 4,000 views each at about a nickel per view. They've been ideal for exposure to new people within our area.

Stick Out with Handwritten Notes

I would say that my favorite marketing advice is to write thank you notes. I was thinking going the high-tech route when contacting people will be the path to take. I was wrong. People are very receptive to receiving handwritten letters and thank-you notes. It sounds silly and easy, but this old-school technique seems to set me apart from my competition. Very few people are achieving this anymore. In real estate, you need any advantage you could get.

Google Ads

The most effective marketing tactics that generates new customers the real deal estate agents and brokerages is Google Ads remarketing. A fairly new feature provided by remarketing is the capability to target people who recently visited specific websites and/or have typed in specific queries on Google. That way, you can easily target people who recently looked for "sell house," "buy house," or "Realtor" and people who visited multiple listing service (MLS) listings and real estate websites, including those of the competitors.

To create that targeting list, go to the Google Ads Campaign dashboard, create a remarketing list centered on interests, and add a list of website URLs and keywords. After this, your advertising banners will likely be served to people that are currently enthusiastic about buying or selling houses individuals who have visited these sites or searched for these keywords and certainly will drive qualified traffic in your region to your site.

Increase Your Network

Besides advertising on StreetEasy, Trulia, and Zillow and sending out monthly newsletters, my top strategy continues to be the personal touch. I host a monthly happy hour open bar in New York City and invite my top clients and their friends and families. It's a terrific way to increase your network organically, and I've gotten a number of my best sales clients that way. I strongly recommend it.

Target Serious Leads

One to generate leads system i love a whole lot is changing the message from "what's your home worth?" to "see exacltly what the home's selling price would be instantly when we put it on the market." This removes the lookie-loos who want to know very well what their investment is really worth so that you are more likely to get somebody wanting to sell and wants to know the price tag of the home. This will drive the prospect to an automated valuation model (AVM) lead capture landing page that could instantly provide them with what their asking price will be centered on active homes currently available on the market in their neighborhood.

Make your own Reference to Video Emails

It's an indisputable fact in 2019, video is king. Agents who are using video to promote their business are crushing it while those who don't are getting left within the dust. For those who have e-mail marketing campaigns set up but aren't converting leads, check out BombBomb that will help you create personalized videos, insert them to your marketing emails, and track engagement.

Host an Annual Party for Clients

As a Realtor, the answer to building a book of company is building relationships. To that end, our realty outfit always throws an annual Carvel ice cream gathering.

The strategy is definitely a huge success as every year we build relationships with real people when you look at the neighborhood and also project our brand while making families happy with free ice cream. I could count several dozen deals we have closed through the years that directly flow from our annual frozen dessert extravaganza.

Harness the ability of Cold Calling

While there are many strategies [to real estate marketing], a recent trend has been the revival for the old marketing way of cold calling. New technology software has managed to make it easier than ever before for a genuine estate investor, agent, or broker to cold call with relative ease. For instance, a cloud-based service called Mojo Dialer will call three cell phone numbers at a time, allowing you to make 300 phone calls in an hour. It's also built to adhere to federal telemarketing rules so that you don't get fined.

Discovery has it that you can get about a 3% to 4% lead conversion rate [when cold-calling], so if you ensure it is a habit of calling for at the very least an hour or so each day, you may likely generate a few leads every day, which equates to sales on a regular basis. Buying lists and skip tracing [locating a person's whereabouts] the records for telephone numbers can cost between 25 cents to $1 per record depending on the services you use. So, if you spend $1,000 on generating an inventory, then diligently call the individuals regarding the list, you are likely to extract 30 to 40 leads and hopefully convert 1 or 2 of those leads into sales.

Use Strategic PR to construct Authority

While many agents think PR is one thing that only celebrities and titans of industry can afford, very few realize they can do it themselves — for free. Mike Fabbri uses sites like Help a Reporter Out (HARO) to pitch his expertise in real estate to journalists interested in sources. In exchange, he gets his name in the press plus the chance to get a link back once again to his website, that will be perfect for SEO.

Craft a Personalized Message for Your Buyers

I've found the most effective results come from an individual message within my voice. When you write your message, remember the following points:

Result in the message about them, They don't worry about you, so let them know how you can assist them to as soon as possible.

Be clear if a seller just isn't sure what you want them to complete, they'll never call you.

Suit your message to your seller

Make your message short and sweet In our fast-paced world, people rarely read all of their email; unsolicited mail often hits the trash can. If you prefer your message to be heard, allow it to be short.

Use Retargeting Campaigns to Drive Website Traffic

A robust method to strengthen your marketing is to set up retargeting campaigns. The concept is always to craft great ad copy that directs visitors to a dedicated landing page or a single-property website utilizing the listing you're marketing. The ad follows your site visitors across the internet and social media marketing, helping you redirect the traffic back once again to your internet site when they're readier to touch base.

Host Local Neighborhood Tours

With regards to great marketing, nothing beats the personal engagement which comes from hosting a fun event for the sphere. Even better why not host a meeting that shows off your personal love and expert knowledge about your farm area?

Luxury Manhattan real estate professional Jeff Goodman does exactly that. Goodman organizes regular walking tours of historic Manhattan neighborhoods for his sphere. Since he hires a professional tour guide when it comes to events, he generally gets 70 or more people to attend each tour.

Choose the Right Farm Area

Maximize the impact of these real estate marketing ideas by choosing the right farm area to establish yourself as a local expert and close more deals. To do so, research the typical age and income of local residents in addition to area amenities, and gain a comprehensive comprehension of your farm area's sales prices, turnover rate, and competition. When you select the right farm area, establish your presence with direct mailers, door hangers, and advertising.

Start an immediate Marketing Campaign

Postcards are an eye-catching and affordable solution to directly market to home buyers and homeowners in your farm area. You need to use direct mailers to market a nearby property to homeowners in a specific neighborhood, share statistics about recently sold properties, or promote your neighborhood real estate office.

Write a Killer Real Estate Newsletter

Once you opt to incorporate a drip email campaign into the real estate online strategy, create killer email newsletters. Relating to Outbound Engine, the subject line is the very first thing potential clients will discover, so use a powerful subject line to fully capture the eye of the readers. Email newsletters also needs to be according to a visually appealing template and include a call to action (CTA) that engages readers and converts leads into clients.

Create a New & Eye-catching Logo

Believe it or not, your logo the most important elements of your individual brand. A fantastic logo often helps propel you forward while a bad logo isn't going to help you attract more leads.

According to Patrick Sanders, creative director the real deal estate marketing powerhouse 1000watt, a great logo should "signal something exciting and new a note to your greater world that the organization is always changing and getting better. [Your work as an agent] should reflect that energy."

Master Your Elevator Pitch

Imagine you were given $5 million to market your business with a 30-second ad through the Super Bowl. What can you say? If this real question is causing you to be scratching your head, you need to work with your elevator pitch. A 30-second-or-less speech that shows off your specific skills and experience offers value and can end up producing more leads.

Use SEO to push Traffic to Your Website

SEO is a sensible way to use your business content to boost website visitors and expand the reach of one's marketing. Certain keywords like "houses for sale," "MLS," and "for sale by owner" or "FSBO" have higher SEO value than many other terms. Optimize your on line content much more with keywords which are extremely local, like "Prospect Heights townhouse," in the place of general keywords like "real estate on the market."

Create a Client Testimonial Packet

Client testimonials are a good solution to show potential home purchasers that you're well-established in your farm area. On its blog, idxcentral.com suggests ensuring you've got informative testimonials by asking clients targeted **q**uestions like, "What made you decide on me as your real estate professional?" Along with counting on clients to provide testimonials, touch base via SurveyMonkey or Yelp to solicit reviews. You should be certain to share positive testimonials via your site and social media.

Create Viral Infographics to fairly share on Social Media

Infographics take useful data and present them in an appealing and easy-to-read format. If you're on any Pinterest or Facebook real estate groups, you've likely seen and shared a large number of infographics already. At Fit Small Company, we use an instrument called Venngage to create great-looking infographics.

Share a Viral Real Estate Video

Videos that go viral via social media are nevertheless very popular. If you can capture someone's attention with a funny or insightful clip, it is possible to reach a wider audience through the effectiveness of social shares. Most people enjoy sharing entertaining videos on Twitter and with family. Regardless if the viewers isn't your target, they may send the video to a person who is.

The perfect real estate marketing ideas depend on your market, firm, and preferred lead management tools. Maximizing your online presence, sharing videos, and creating SEO-optimized content are effective tools for marketing your agency. Developing a marketing strategy also allows you to streamline to generate leads and client outreach so that you can concentrate on selling houses. Make sure to utilize the tips above to really make the much of your marketing efforts.

SOME MORE OUTSIDE-THE-BOX REAL ESTATE MARKETING IDEAS

Unique. Original. Remarkable. It's tough to develop real estate marketing ideas day in and day out that meet each of these criteria — especially once you spend a lot of your own time on the road meeting with clients and leads.

Sometimes, however, the best fix for marketing fatigue is thinking away from box and identifying ways your primary marketing channels – website, SEO, email marketing, paid advertising and social networking content – can differentiate your agency or brokerage through the competition. .

Below is, creative real estate marketing suggestions to help promote your agency and generate more leads. Whether you're just starting or are a professional realtor trying to attract new business, this guide will give you the tips and materials needed to build an effective marketing campaign.

Build a Rock Solid Marketing Foundation

The prosperity of your realtor industry relies on how well your internet marketing funnel attracts new house buyers. 44% of all of the home buyers and 99% of Millennials go to the Internet first when finding properties on the market. As a realtor, you need a professional website if you be prepared to increase revenue as time passes.

Home buyers expect *q*uality while they search for homes therefore the realtor that best fits their demands. Your internet site should showcase your home listings, brand and expertise. Tools that help you stick out include:
- Branded messaging and images
- Responsive design

- IDX integration
- Blog content
- Lead capture landing pages
- **Area** pages

Your brand provides website visitors immediate understanding about who you really are, your expertise and how you're positioned to help them. A responsive realtor website means your pages show perfectly no real matter what type of device (desktop, laptop, tablet or cell phone) your prospects use when accessing your content.

Publish a nearby market quiz on the real estate website

In the event that you've ever checked out BuzzFeed before, then chances are you know people want to take quizzes on virtually any subject. Test your audience with a quick, multiple-choice quiz on something of great interest. See if they know things like which famous people was raised in the area and tidbits about your town's history. The questions or topics can even be created around broader subjects unrelated to your market, like music, movies, or some other element of pop culture.

If you want to function as the ultimate resource for your leads, however, a thought-provoking quiz regarding the ins and outs of selling or buying a home, such as the one below from Kevin Ho and Jonathan McNarry of San Francisco-based Vanguard Properties, could possibly be your ticket to gaining their confidence.

Think about these quick exams as you of the real estate marketing tools to make use of every now and then — perhaps as part of your marketing with email campaign. You might even create a contest round the quiz: Require people who take it to fill out a lead capture form by the end and give the winner something special card to a local restaurant or cafe.

Offer Home Valuations to Capture Seller Leads

Potential sellers need to know simply how much their home may be worth. Integrate a home valuation tool to your website and capture seller leads.

The following is a typical example of what this may seem like on your own site

Valuation report

Once your visitor enters their address, they're prompted to deliver their current email address as well as other information so that you can view their home valuation report. After they provide this information, you've got an innovative new seller lead to contact.

Just because they will not sign up through email, you are able to follow-up through regular mail since your home valuation software has recently captured the home address.

Film an explainer video that goes into detail regarding the agency

Differentiate your business from other agents in your market with real estate explainer videos. Don a black turtleneck and explain your services as you were Steve Jobs (rest in peace). Pretend to be a political candidate and pitch people on why you're the right person to do the job. Heck, even take a full page out from the "Arrested Development" playbook and mock those awful 1-800 lawyer commercials.

These videos are traditionally meant to be serious, because they relay your value proposition and the thing that makes your agency successful and worth hiring. But as noted, personality plays a large role when you look at the decision-making of buyers and sellers, so have a blast while still getting across the info that's needed for consumers to know about your brand.

Provide a no cost moving truck

That is an original solution to get noticed in your local market. Invest in a moving truck along with your branding regarding the side. Offer it to your customers when they purchase or sell their property. Your online business benefits from additional branding and advertising each time your clients place the truck to make use of.

Get creative when clients don't need your moving truck. Go on it to home shows. Park it in elements of town that benefit you with high volumes of vehicle and pedestrian traffic.

Answer buyer/seller questions in your blog

An effective way to get ideas for blog content will be identify *q*uestions your target market is asking. Two tools assist you in finding these lists of *q*uestions:

•Answer The General Public
•People Also Ask

Answer The Public is a free tool that generates a summary of *q*uestions according to your keyword search. For instance, if you type in "los angeles homes", the *q*uestions received from this search can sometimes include:

•Must I buy a los angeles home?
•Simply how much will it be to get a los angeles home?

People Also Ask is a free feature inside a Google search:

People also ask

A third tool for finding interesting searches to target is a chrome extension called Keywords Everywhere. It gives you related searches (along with estimated search volume) to any Google search:

Keywords Everywhere

Add some flavor to your real estate video marketing.

Sending a contact to your contacts to wish them a happy holiday likely won't nurture your leads through the sales funnel like blog posts and promotional email messages do. With that said, getting in the spirit for widely celebrated goings-on locally or nationally can humanize your brand.

Have a look at what the group at Modern Life Realty and ERA Justin Realty teams accomplished in listed here recordings: The former takes a normal video marketing technique and turns it on its head by talking to the camera with ... well ... whatever it is the featured gentleman is donning. Meanwhile, the latter hops on the "Call Me Maybe" bandwagon (which has long since been abandoned, but that is another story) and capitalizes on its fifteen minutes of fame.

Both took a chance, that is that which you have to do from time to time together with your real estate online strategy, as these tactics can often pay big dividends.

Together with these outlandish videos, consider conducting "man-on-the-street" interviews as well. The subjects of the videos don't need certainly to pertain to your business if not real estate as a whole. You could question them philosophical questions, like what this is of life is, or inquire further for his or her thoughts on an area college or professional sports team.

Develop a blog post or video series highlighting great area restaurants and entertainment.

Though property price, size, style, and features will be the top considerations for the modern home buyer, residing in a residential district with plentiful food and entertainment options is an ever more important aspect as well.

Yelp, TripAdvisor, and a wealth of other websites offer up reviews and facts about movie theaters, restaurants, and similar businesses. However these portals have an issue: they are able to take forever to sort through merely to find a well-written review or locate the best information. That's for which you, the all-knowing real estate professional, comes into play.

Develop a number of blog posts and/or videos that provides home buyers interested in your market the lowdown on the premier eateries and establishments in your area.

Finding these locales shouldn't be a challenge simply think of your own favorite places to see a play or grab a bite with friends. Then, jot down why you adore those places and share your opinions utilizing the world, like Realtor Michelle Calkins does in her blog post series and Realtor David Gonzalez does into the YouTube clip.

Order unique business cards that stick out.

Business cards will never walk out style. You'll also have in-person meetings and meet-ups with buyers, sellers, and other industry professionals, meaning it is vital to have your information readily available to generally share using them. But a boring card that lists your online business name and contact information when you look at the smallest, plainest font won't be memorable.

Take a risk and order some original business cards few have likely seen before. For example, take a good look at these fine examples featured on ViralNova that use the concept to the next level.

Research the best business card creation services on the market and attempt to find one that proposes to develop distinct versions like the one above that will get individuals to remember you long after your conversation with them ends. It may seem like a little item to target so much of your attention on, but marketing for real estate agents will continue to evolve and start to become more competitive because of the day, so seemingly minor touches such as this are able to keep you top-of-mind.

Incorporate your furry friend into several of your real estate listing photos.

Though its not all home buyer will take care of seeing a cute French bulldog or Grumpy Cat look-alike throughout a property they tour on your own real estate website, chances are the occasional photo featuring pets won't turn fully off consumers and may even appeal to your buyers you're interested in.

Use your pup or cat, or borrow one from a family member or friend, to feature in your listing shots. (Side note: If you somehow convince your canine pal to have in the relaxed pose due to the fact one above, as featured in this Curbed article, you really need to take up a side business as your dog whisperer).

Use Instagram Stories

The answer to building your brand on Instagram (and all sorts of social networking platforms) is to become great at getting your followers to engage to you. Instagram Stories provide you with an approach for generating engagement and gaining brand recognition in the act.

One method to use Instagram Stories is always to run a giveaway or contest. Direct followers to take screenshots while they listen directly into your IG Live segment and direct message you those images. Choose a winner and present them something fun or helpful (a free book about qualifying for a financial loan, for instance).

Cross pollinate your social networking channels using the above method. Utilize it together with your Facebook Lives or tweets to get your FB and Twitter followers to realize you on Instagram.

Devise a fun game to accompany awards shows or televised events

Ever see publications, bloggers, and brands share "drinking games" for events like the Academy Awards additionally the Super Bowl? Participate in and produce your own personal form of a casino game (of this drinking variety or something different is your decision). You can even create an interactive or printable bingo chart, of sorts, (see The Wall Street Journal's interactive take below) for people to make use of during these events to check out in case the amusing insights and predictions come true. Brand this marketing collateral along with your logo to get those who partake in your game to remember where they first got it.

Post ideas and strategies for homeowners, buyers, and sellers in Reddit.

Before you can get all flustered wondering how Reddit will help your real estate marketing (or what Reddit even is), just know that the website isn't simply the "front page of the internet," as it promotes itself to be. You will find endless quantities of "subreddit" forum boards on the website dedicated to the essential specific topics on the planet including homeownership, home buying, and home selling. Find ones by which people looking to purchase or sell properties need sage wisdom and where homeowners are searching for advice regarding their mortgages or tax tips.

Capitalize on the rise in popularity of the latest internet memes.

You may be thinking memes are simply another internet distraction — one that keeps you against completing important tasks, like segmenting real estate leads in your customer relationship management (CRM) database or scheduling meetings with prospective clients. On the contrary, though: Memes offer a (dare we say) fun real estate marketing tactic that is at the moment taking off with agents and certainly will get some laughs from your own audience.

The next you observe that a (politically correct and totally appropriate-for-work) meme is making the rounds online, try to come up with ways to use it on Facebook, Twitter, Instagram, or Pinterest (like Realtor Paul Fernandez's board above), and even on your blog. A post titled "10 Feelings All Home Buyers Have throughout the Process" filled with memes could be your key to connecting with your targeted demographic.

Fabricate mock logos for your agency that replicate famous ones.

If you're a large fan of a specific television show, incorporate the famous typeface and/or imagery connected with one (or maybe more) of this series with your personal real estate logo. Make it timely by sharing a message with your list featuring your new, short-term branding and an email about when the new season premieres. There are many directions you can take this faux-go (have it?), so find a well-known pop culture design or symbol you can mess around with for your own real estate marketing. Just be sure not to ever utilize it in too many promotional materials (the very last thing you would like is to find a cease-and-desist from billion-dollar entities).

Send Handwritten Notes

You have the opportunity to offer your prospects and clients a unique experience once they open a mailed envelope and discover a handwritten note inside.

Combine this strategy with all the home valuation tool mentioned previously. Send handwritten notes to your home valuation leads that failed to enter their email address.

Create a referral system

While you create your online presence and leadflow, don't forget about getting referrals from happy clients. One of the easiest ways to get referrals would be to simply ask. Concentrate on providing your prospects a smooth transition for the entire real estate process and then inquire further who they know.

Staying dedicated to providing ongoing tips and helpful content to email subscribers will foster more referrals. Send periodic content to your clients providing you with house owner tips. This high touch follow-up keeps you "top of mind" when past customers hear that friends and family are looking to buy a house.

Real Estate Marketing Niches

- •Real Estate Branding Ideas
- •Real Estate SEO Tips
- •Real Estate Advertisement Ideas
- •Real Estate Social Media Ideas
- •Real Estate Listing Marketing Ideas
- •Real Estate Email Ideas
- •Real Estate Social Video Marketing Ideas
- •Offline Real Estate Marketing Ideas

Real Estate Branding Ideas

Develop a solid real estate agent bio and add it to your About Page.

When leads find your brand online, they must be able to get a powerful sense of your professional qualifications and personality. Craft a real estate bio that leads will cherish, detailing your experiences, values, and interests, and place it prominently on the 'About Me' page of one's website.

You may be your brand, which means that your personal photograph should exude an amiable demeanor and elevate your brand with an expert look.

Hire a specialist photographer who is able to provide advice on positioning, and who is able to ensure that the final product is crisp and presentable in many different formats. If you're low on funds at the beginning of your job, you can even choose to take one all on your own that looks professional.

Develop a value proposition.

Should you want to be a fruitful agent, you must not have only uni**q**ue characteristics that set you apart through the competition, you should certainly define what those uni**q**ue features mean to your clients, leads, and community.

A **q**uick value proposition should exhibit your value and strengths as a representative. This statement are going to be reused in your marketing materials over and over again.

Prepare a 30-second pitch to use when talking to new leads.

If you created a value proposition (above), you are able to think about a pitch as something very similar. But how things are keep reading paper doesn't necessarily translate well to personal interactions.

In your initial conversations with leads, you need to be capable of making a **q**uick but powerful statement that conveys you're a knowledgeable agent that knows the market better than anyone. Once you've created your pitch, practice it out loud.

Ac**q**uire some swag printed with your branding.

Brand exposure in your town might help increase your business. Get items like calendars, pens, keychains, and notepads, and have now your name, logo, and email address printed on them to pass off to clients or at local events.

A company's online star rating is the no. 1 factor used by consumers to evaluate a company.

Online reviews have a prominent presence in search engines, have a sizable effect on your business's reputation, and tend to be an important source of lead referrals. Seize control of the brand by requesting online reviews from good past clients, and then make it easy in order for them to post in multiple places.

Ask your best former clients for testimonials.

Happy past clients are your best brand ambassadors. Their opinions and feedback on your own site will give your brand social clout. Approach a few of your very best former clients and get if they would offer feedback for a testimonial. Written is good, but testimonials with photos or video are even better.

Have an original signature item or look.

Many agents have an exceptional look, whether it's a color they wear often, a method of dress, a hat, or hairstyle (our VP of Marketing, Seth Price is known for his pink-hued pants). Develop a confident, distinctive factor for the personal brand this is certainly recognizable and memorable.

Set up squeeze pages or lead capture forms on your own site for lead gen.

Lead capture forms are excellent how to secure lead information to help you take communication into the hands. Put up squeeze pages after someone clicks on a residential property advertisement, or maybe before someone gets all the information about a residential property on the site.

Additionally, it's also wise to have optional lead capture forms on each website page for leads thinking about getting more information. Forms should ask for name, phone number, email, and also a location where someone can pose a question.

Place your contact information on every page of your website.

With to generate leads being one of your top priorities, your contact information shouldn't be hidden or only using one page of your website. Prominently showcase your contact info on every page to make it easy for contributes to reach out.

Include beautiful royalty-free local imagery.

With regards to building a good online experience for the website visitors, nothing does the work *q*uite in addition to local photography. Getting usage of royalty-free images could be difficult, but use one of the numerous online and local resources to get great shots of the local area.

Give leads expense information and calculators.

Most clients have financial *q*uestions. Create a document you are able to share with leads to assist them to calculate their expenses, before, during, and after a sale.

Use calls to action to boost user engagement.

Many people place calls to action at the end of a blog post, you should make use of them various other regions of your internet site as well:

• sidebar prompts to sign up for your newsletters

• a homepage area asking folks to get in touch with you

• or near the top of lead capture forms so folks could possibly get more information on a residential property

Effective calls to action include enticing copy that get a person to do this on the site.

Add testimonials to your homepage.

When you've re**q**uested testimonials from your happiest and most vocal clients, showcase them on your homepage to leverage the social proof they provide.

Add social sharing buttons to your site.

Social sharing is a massive section of generating referral traffic and building brand recognition online. This procedure should always be possible for your website visitors so everyone can click them and share your articles **q**uickly with reduced effort. Many website themes carry these as standard, or you can choose to install a plugin for the site.

Write and publish content on the blog regularly.

Successful inbound marketing starts with consistent content creation. This enhances your quest engine optimization, generates traffic, and provides real value to your customers.

Consistency is crucial in blogging: You should be prepared to publish between 2–5 blog posts each week on your own market, listings, area details, and real estate statistics. See these 101 blog post ideas for inspiration.

Develop guides for buyers and sellers.

Just about any lead you encounter will probably have a lot of **q**uestions regarding buying or selling, which means you're probably answering similar **q**uestions over repeatedly and scrambling to find resources that can help them.

Make your own downloadable or printable guides you can easily give to leads such as lots of information on processes and expectations.

Vary post types.

Not every bit of content has got to be a long-form piece. In fact, most readers love variety. Create a mix of written blogs, ebooks, infographics, videos, photos, lists, etc.

Curate content from other sources to incorporate on your own site.

Its not all bit of content on the site has to be completely original. Effectively curating content from other sites, crediting the first source, and adding your very own perspective makes content creation simple and *q*uick.

Use analytics to operate a vehicle your marketing.

Whether it's a bit of content that gets high traffic, a listing that gets high time-on-site statistics, or an influx in referrals from a specific blogger, monitor your site analytics and visitor behavior to ascertain where you should focus your marketing.

Real Estate Listing Marketing Ideas

Optimize listing pages.

Optimize your listing pages with local keywords, proper address formatting, and appropriately sized photos, in addition to necessary links.

Feature top listings from the home page

Your house page is normally one of the most visited pages in your website. Make the most of this traffic by offering your best listings here.

Construct great real estate listing copy.

Great writing could make or break a listing's potential. The smallest amount details won't do the trick if you would like have the best leads while offering. Write great real estate listing copy with interesting adjectives and descriptions that entice readers.

Make your listings look their best.

Stage properties and hire a professional photographer to fully capture the very best angles of every room.

Dedicate blog posts or landing pages to showcase your listings at length.

A dedicated post or landing page for a list makes it possible to build a robust marketing campaign for a property (beyond just the listing page).

Add more in-depth descriptions, photos, video, and information on the area to higher pitch the property. So that you can attract organic traffic, optimize the post with:

•hyper-local keywords
•address names
•and property type keywords

Share the blog along with your network while you would an everyday blog post.

Advertise listings in a separate newsletter to your leads and clients.

Leverage email's great ROI by making use of your newsletter to advertise your listings to clients. Keep your message fairly brief and to-the-point, adding in alluring subject lines and headers, a few striking photos, descriptive detail, and a hyperlink to your listing or website landing page when it comes to property.

Create video presentations for your listings.

Photos are anticipated included in listings, but video can build a fuller experience for the leads and provide them a more in-depth perspective in the property. Create professional property videos for priority listings to generate a host of great interest.

Post listing all about every social networking outlet.

Listings on your own website are great, but let your followers know about new featured listings by posting them on each social media site.

Develop listing boards on Pinterest.

Pinterest is a great platform to create mood or informational boards around listings.

Include pictures of your property, scenes and highlights regarding the area, and general advice and tips for buyers. Make sure to include your contact information and links into the listing page or squeeze page for the listing.

Real Estate Social Media Marketing Ideas
Social media marketing

Your brand must have a stronger presence on social media, as they are a significant driver of successful marketing campaigns and referral traffic.

Even although you don't currently use all of them, it's good practice to secure usernames on every platform just in case you choose to use them later, including Facebook, Twitter, Google+, LinkedIn, Pinterest, YouTube, SlideShare, Foursquare and Instagram. If possible, make use of the same account name across all platforms.

Create custom social media bios for every single platform.

Every social media site is unique: Their users interact differently and expect different sorts of personality (think a hilarious video on Facebook versus a vocation advice article on LinkedIn).

Additionally, each platform provides you with different amounts of space to publish a bio. Write social networking bios that be noticeable on each platform but still sound consistent across all of your social media marketing channels.

Invite relatives and buddies to such as your pages or follow you.

Every page starts with zero, so let your personal network to offer your web social brands a boost.

Invite friends, family, colleagues, and past clients to like or follow your professional pages so you can build an instantaneous following (and they also can easily see and share what you post).

Add social media retargeting tags to your internet site

As you understand that most people to your site won't convert to customers immediately, it's important to utilize retargeting. And also this applies to email leads who don't convert straight away.

Retargeting is a way for which you place an item of code, called a pixel, on the website pages. This then allows you to "retarget", or "remarket" to those people across different social networking platforms.

As an example, a Facebook pixel on your own site allows you to place an ad in the front of these visitors the very next time each goes on Facebook. Can be done the same along with other channels like Twitter, YouTube, Instagram and LinkedIn.

This marketing method lets you re-engage prospects no matter where they're going. It builds your brand and creates awareness regarding the services every time a past site visitor sees your offerings.

Post regularly on each social media marketing platform.

Social media marketing is only as potent as how it is used.

Successful agents using social media know it re*q*uires a regular posting to build an audience that may engage with you. This means posting just about every day on your core social media sites.

Use our post to find out more in what types of content work best on each social site.

Include social follow buttons on your own website.

You should ensure it is more than easy for folks to get and follow your social media accounts. Whether or not it's in your header, footer, or sidebar, ensure your icons are prominent on the page.

Showcase your savvy with video.

Video specials that offer your real estate knowledge, advice to buyers and sellers, or give in-depth previews of listings can deliver a significant return in your marketing.

Additionally, optimizing your YouTube videos can boost the SEO of the content.

Get a social media scheduler.

Being an enthusiastic poster on social media marketing doesn't have to mean being glued to your computer or laptop every minute of the day. Many posts, like blog posts, announcements, property details, and general advice could be scheduled in advance using automated systems like Hootsuite, Buffer, or Edgar.

Generate slideshows.

Multimedia presentations made out of content on your own website can build readership from audiences who prefer visuals to plain text. Publishing slideshows on platforms like SlideShare puts your articles right in front of potentially tens and thousands of users.

Join a Twitter discussion

Twitter is a superb platform to activate with other professionals or leads. Follow major real estate related topics by searching relevant hashtags and offer thoughts or pose questions.

You may host your own personal Twitter chat, in which case you'll need to advertise it to your leads via email and social networking, allowing them to know how to engage with you through that time and energy to get their questions answered.

Develop or join groups, and begin discussions there to create thought leadership.

Many discussions and coalitions are made within social media groups. Join some to create your network, or create your own to build a resource where you are able to offer advice.

Run a contest through social networking.

Contests may be a good way to come up with leads. Use social networking to host a contest, and gives a prize, like a present card to an area business or a free of charge consultation.

Publish new, original thoughtful articles on LinkedIn.

LinkedIn now allows one to create thoughtful articles inside their publisher platform. Applying this platform can get your ideas right in front of a huge number of readers.

Real Estate Advertisement Ideas Discover ways to set up advertising campaigns.

Whether it's for search engines or social media, learn the basics of setting goals, understanding pricing, and setting up campaigns.

Set your targets for the focused keywords you need to target additionally the types of customers who does result in the most *q*ualified leads. You'll use this information later when setting up campaigns.

Whilst the length and scope of the copy depends on platform, most ads contain a value proposition and proactive approach. Write these early and present yourself a few choices to test against one another.

Choose a vendor to setup campaigns for you.

Setting up, monitoring, and tracking promotional initiatives needs time to work and lots of advertising savvy.

Agents who want to maximize the impact of these ads should make use of an established company where they are able to have a person oversee their campaigns and supply guidance on how they've been performing.

Creating an ad budget.

Understand the factors which will impact the investment you need to make to get the return you're hoping for. Then, calculate your PPC ROI predicated on your budget.

Use social media marketing.

Social media marketing advertising can place your message in the front of targeted users. Major networks like Facebook, Twitter, Google+, and LinkedIn offer choices to place your message in front of these large audiences.

Develop captivating graphics for ads.

The strongest ads have visual elements to attract users in. Create custom photos or video to pair along with your ads and maximize their potential.

Advertise in high-audience newsletters.

There are popular consumer-facing real estate brands that send out regular newsletters. Advertising there can place your ad in front of a large number of readers, but it's far better go with hyper-local newsletters.

Create a dedicated splash page attached to your ad.

Should you want to increase to generate leads from your ad, a click should lead to a website landing page in which you provide more worthiness to your lead (based on the content associated with the original ad), as well as a lead capture form.

Create custom media around featured properties.

For featured listings, create custom images, graphics, and video to promote the most effective components of a certain property.

Targeted video advertising of single properties.

Target specific users with YouTube advertising by showcasing captivating video of single properties.

Layer on retargeting across key channels

Identify the social media marketing channels most critical to your online business and re-engage your warm audience. For instance, target non-converting website visitors the very next time they visit Facebook, LinkedIn, Twitter or Instagram.

Real Estate SEO
Put up a Google My Business page

Google My Business lets you manage and control how your real estate industry appears in Google Search and Maps listings.

Filling out your NAP (name, address and phone number) profile completely can help you show up properly in Google's 3-pack map listing:

LA RE agents

The main reason you want your agency to exhibit up in the 3-pack is simply because searchers pay attention to the visual aspect of the:

- map
- ratings
- prominent website and directions links
- the decision button on mobile devices

Getting your site placed in this top 3 listing area improves your possibilities to attract quality local leads.

Submit site to major aggregators

Most of the data spread throughout the neighborhood search ecosystem is handled because of the major data aggregators. Localeze, Factual, Acxiom and Infogroup would be the four major aggregators that publish local business information to social media, search engines, directories and review websites.

Submitting your details to these aggregators increases your chances that Google as well as other search engines take your business seriously. You certainly will gain an aggressive advantage when you've listed your agency correctly, while other local real estate professionals and brokers have neglected to do this.

Ensure consistent NAP across all online properties

Employ a consistent approach when filling out company information during the major aggregators or directories. A large part to upping your local search engine rankings would be to make sure that every listing is consistent with the second.

As an example, each listing needs to have your organization name, address, contact number and website listed a similar. This prevents duplicate listings and avoids confusion as internet search engine algorithms regulate how to rank your company.

More specifically, any online property that lists your

NAP is named a citation. Google and Bing consider NAP inconsistencies across citations as an adverse search signal. Should your business has 3 similar listings inside one directory, for instance, the search engines don't know which one is accurate.

This creates doubt in the algorithm regarding how trustworthy the company is. The end result is a diminished search ranking.

When you consider that Google's search market share is close to 90%, you want to be sure you do everything possible to increase your presence there

Set up schema

Schema enables you to mark up elements in your site in a manner that helps Google determine what the data means. Through schema markups, you will get the ability to tell Google just how to attractively present your information.

For example, take a look at how you can list your upcoming open house directly into the search results and inquire yourself about the quality of leadflow that results from this marketing method:

Conduct key word research

Your real estate advertising campaign should include a thorough policy for taking advantage of keyword searches employed by future site visitors. You can find 3 basic kinds of real estate keywords to research and employ:

- Primary (ex, newport beach homes)
- Secondary (ex, orange county real estate)
- Long-tail (ex, tips for buying real estate in costa mesa)

These areas are further segmented with regards to:
- buyer intent (realtor near me, santa ana houses on the market, etc)
- sort of sale (luxury vs foreclosure)
- property type (house vs condo)
- location (oceanfront vs lake)
- Information gathering stage (do I need a realtor, house buying tips, etc)

Of course, you want to attract qualified prospects thinking of buying now. Don't underestimate the effectiveness of attracting site leads that are when you look at the information gathering stage, however. Warm these prospects up, get them to trust you and then benefit once they decide this is the time to start out thinking of buying their next bit of real estate.

Several tools exist to assist you research your following set of real estate keywords:
- Ahrefs (paid tool)
- ahrefs
- Ubersuggest (free tool)
- ubersuggest Re
- Answer the general public (free tool)
- answerpublicRE

Build local landing pages

A proper estate sq̄ueeze page is a single page on your site which allows you to talk with a particular segment of your target audience.

For example, if you're targeting a keyword such as for example "guide to buying Phoenix real estate", you'll get much more leads pointing your visitors to a landing page offering a free guide for purchasing real estate in Phoenix than pointing them to a generic home page.

Since multiple landing pages causes a 120% rise in leadflow, it is important to master how to make use of the various real estate splash page methods.

Collect reviews on major 3rd party review sites

There was a primary correlation amongst the amount of reviews your agency collects and the local search engine rankings. In fact, ranking signals account fully for 15.44% of Google's local search rankings

Local search factors

Your interaction with reviews is vital. Google states specifically to their Google My Business help page which they not only pay attention to reviews that are positive in terms of ranking sites, but that your particular interaction with reviewers is a factor.

Build local backlinks

Increasing the number of other sites linking to your real estate website will enhance your search engine rankings

Monitor backlinks

The cause of it is that more incoming links to your internet site improves your domain authority and so, overall keyword rankings across your entire site.

Real Estate Email Marketing Ideas

Create an email signature with essential details.

Your email signature should include your complete name, phone number, email address, and website address that links straight to your internet site. Not just is this an easy way to produce your information, it means that in case your email is forwarded, the recipient will discover all your brand details as well.

Put up email sign-up forms in your site to cultivate your recipient list.

You can only get a good return on your investment in email when you yourself have a considerable recipient list. Use on-site sign-up forms with effective calls to action to have readers to join up.

Put up autoresponders for thank-yous if not immediately available.

Whether it's late during the night or you're away at a conference, set up autoresponder messages to let clients and leads know you're not immediately available but that you'll get back into them at the earliest opportunity.

The exact same goes for messages to those who download a reference from your own site or RSVP to an event.

Construct responsive email templates that look good on every device.

Email templates also come in all sizes and shapes, you ought to be using a newsletter template with responsive design and clean layout.

Segment your email list.

If you would like give very personal experiences to your leads, segment your email list predicated on client personas and needs. Then, target communications with details pertinent to each client.

Personalize emails.

Including a recipient's name as well as other details from your interactions can make emails feel more personal and certainly will deepen their trust.

Use storytelling and imagery to boost engagement.

Include effective storytelling elements and videos or images to increase click-through and conversion rates for the emails.

Add social media accounts and share buttons to your emails.

Increase cross-platform engagement by encouraging users to fairly share your email content right on their social media marketing accounts with share buttons put into your email. Use a modern template to obtain these features.

Adapt your email calls to action according to needs.

Make use of your list segmentation and lead tracking to figure out the very best proactive approach to supply each lead as a next thing, whether that's getting new contributes to subscribe to your newsletter or getting a client close to sale to download a closing checklist.

Develop a message course for leads.

Your leads are most likely facing similar roadblocks or questions. Increase email engagement by offering an exclusive email course to go over various real estate issues, offering a fresh tip each day or week.

Offline Real Estate Marketing Ideas

Establish partnerships with geographic area businesses.

Develop relationships with local businesses and ask for to place your real estate cards or listing information at their desk or bulletin board.

Sponsor local events.

Local events, churches, schools, and sports events are constantly seeking sponsors. Look into fees in return for brand advertising on booklets, t-shirts, banners, flyers, etc.

Host free seminars on topics concerning buyers or sellers in your area.

Don't just offer value to locals when you have a list in the marketplace. Find areas to host informal sessions to offer your knowledge and advice to locals. Use a sign-in sheet to get information so you can follow up with attendees after.

Advertise your company and listings in local media.

Advertise your brand in local media like newspapers, magazines, radio, television, etc. To have your messaging right in front of local leads.

Take local sponsorships one step further.

Be creative with local sponsorship opportunities: Sponsor the coffee mugs at your local coffee shop, the golf tee boxes at a golf club, or a stand at the local farmers market.

Run an open house.

Develop open houses where you could interact closely with local leads and offer intimate walk-throughs.

Make sure the house is staged well, and offer a lot of

snacks, packets in regards to the property, and free swag together with your company logo. Collect information via an open house sign-in sheet and follow through with leads a single day after your event.

Use custom banners, balloons, and signs to market your open house.

Build brand recognition every time you host an open house by providing signage and other extras. Go the additional mile by putting your name brand or logo to them.

Create a physical high-quality mailer.

Mailers might help get listings and your brand in the possession of of everyone in your community. Use high-gloss paper and sophisticated design to build premier real estate mailers for your area.

Write a consistent column for the local media.

A consistent column in your neighborhood newspaper, magazine, or online blog will help you present your knowledge to an area audience and build recognition in your community. If you're a much better talker, add your thoughts to a regular radio show.

Attend local events and join local meetup groups and associations.

Being a force in the local community means turning up in places where you can build real face-to-face relationships. Use local groups, festivals, or meetings to develop your contact base.

Real Estate Video Promotion Tips and Ideas

Interview happy customers

Person to person recommendations are a powerful method to help prospects understand your value. Take care to interview past customers and permit their words to accomplish the heavy lifting with regards to pointing out of the features of working with you specifically.

Don't forget to enhance your interviews beyond past clients. Interview home inspectors, mortgage brokers, construction company owners along with other people you work with through the entire entire procedure of a house sale.

It's your possibility to show your prospects the positive way everyone you work with looks upon you.

Shoot video tours of most listings

Showing is obviously a lot better than telling. Using listing videos to showcase the properties you have got on the market is one of the most effective how to help prospects see precisely what each property offers them.

This will be a method to get prospects motivated to raise their relationship with you and schedule phone and in-person meetings.

Publish home/buyer educational videos

Educational videos that offer real estate buyers advice are an approach to establish credibility. It is a real estate marketing idea that reveals your expertise and shows prospects exactly how much you're interested in educating them regarding the advantages and pitfalls involved in their purchase decisions.

Focus in on mortgage options, how to save for an advance payment, tax advantages to owning a property, the necessity of inspection reports and other similar topics you know your buyers will benefit from learning about.

Record neighborhood community videos

Create videos that showcase the area and community atmosphere across the homes you sell. Your prospects wish to know they're moving into a safe area with excellent schools, parks and surrounding neighborhoods.

Showcase other homes, businesses, developments, restaurants, shopping areas and other neighborhood features that help your buyers determine what variety of community they're potentially stepping into.

Promote helpful how-to videos

Use helpful "how-to" video content to instruct prospects step-by-step methods to solve challenges or realize important concepts you know they ought to understand throughout the buying experience.

For example, a how-to video that walks a prospect through the method for selecting their realtor goes quite a distance in getting them to see you since the perfect choice.

Add videos to email drip series

Don't forget to include your video content within your email follow-up sequences. Create a welcome drip series so that new subscribers receive videos with your written content.

Promote videos across social media channels

It's important to combine your entire social media platforms into one synergistic real estate advertising campaign. Prevent the tendency to produce videos and use YouTube since the only distribution channel.

Instead, take that content and distribute across Facebook, Instagram, Twitter and any kind of social channel you determine to use as part of your marketing efforts.

HOW TO BUILD A FRUITFUL REAL ESTATE MARKETING CAMPAIGN

Set clear goals

Identify which objectives you'll strive to achieve. Create a strategy and understand what types of habits you will need to grow into.

Are you going to assess the wide range of sales each month? What number of new leads generated every month? Think about which marketing strategy shall help you accomplish each goal.

Use activity goals, too. For example, hone in on a particular quantity of calls in order to make each day. You'll experience pros and cons when marketing your real estate business. Measuring activity helps ensure that you'll continue spending so much time when results haven't shown themselves yet.

Identify your target customer

Marketing always is best suited when its messaging is focused on a certain segment of the overall market. As an example, your marketing will need to speak one method to investors and an entirely different way in the event your target customers are very first time home buyers.

Establish your unique selling proposition

Figuring out your unique selling proposition (USP) identifies how exactly to set yourself aside from other real estate professionals.

Think about the thing that makes you unique. What would you bring towards the table that they don't?

Can it be your experience?

Your personality?

Your knowledge of this area?

Or something else?

How does your USP provide value to your customers and encourage them to work well with you?

Choose marketing channels to reach audience

Decide which marketing channels to use. It's impractical to discover the time for you to use every social media platform available and optimize each channel effectively. Choose where your time and effort will undoubtedly be used best.

Are you going to use an online site? Are you going to blog often? Will you use Facebook, Twitter, YouTube or other social networking option? Find the marketing channels which make the most sense according to your personality as well as other skill-sets.

Define a lead nurturing strategy

Heat up email leads by periodically sending them information that builds trust and reveals your expertise. Send out new blog posts to your newsletter list. Provide your subscribers with neighborhood updates, housing market trends, how-to videos, details about simple tips to qualify for that loan, walk-through videos of the latest listings, etc.

Select tools to make usage of the plan

Make a listing of the tools had a need to put your real estate marketing campaign into action. Determine your email service provider, project management software, event software, website creation software as well as other brand building tools.

Measure performance

Define precise metrics to measure achievement with. Use goals that easily inform you whether you've strike the mark within specific timeframes.

Don't write, "I will increase my lead flow".

Instead, create a goal that says, "I will generate 500 new email subscribers into the month of June." You will be aware for sure at the conclusion of the month whether 500 new leads were generated or perhaps not.

Ready. Set. Market.

As you care able to see, there are lots of ways to market your real estate business.

Invest some time to determine which strategies take advantage sense for you personally and then create your foundation. Focus on the steps that build off of assets you have in place. For example, if you have got a large Facebook following already, try to find tips above that help you maximize that audience.

Then, transfer to other areas that logically build your web site larger. It's very easy to become overwhelmed. The important thing is always to plan out the long-term strategy and then start implementing that plan step-by-step each week.

Finally, make certain your entire real estate strategies revolve around your site. Your site will be your "home" on the net. It's the place where most lead flow and business will come from.

Create your brand. Increase your traffic. Enjoy a steady upsurge in revenue from your own real estate business.

REAL ESTATE TERMS TO KNOW

Having a simple knowledge of important real estate concepts prior to starting the homebuying process will provide you with peace of mind now and may help save you a lot of money in the future. Check out real estate terms you should know before you begin trying to find a home. In the event that you still have questions or will be ready to start touring homes, a Redfin real estate professional will be very happy to help.

Buyer's Agent vs. Listing Agent

You will find usually two agents involved once you buy a property; the "buyer's agent," who represents you, therefore the "listing agent," who represents the home seller. Dual agency occurs when there is certainly only 1 agent representing both sides of this transaction, and it's also something you wish to avoid without exceptions!

Fixed Rate vs. Adjustable Rate Mortgages

Conventional loans include "fixed rate" and "adjustable rate" mortgages. A hard and fast rate mortgage has a predetermined rate of interest for the lifetime of the mortgage; the most typical are for 30 years. A variable rate mortgage has a variable interest rate; the most frequent are for 5, 7, or ten years.

Pre-approval Letter

Before you make an application for a mortgage if not start looking for a home, you ought to get a pre-approval letter through the bank, that will be an estimate of just how much they'll lend you. This letter will help you know what you can afford, and ensures home sellers you will be able to get that loan when needed.

Listings

Real estate professionals frequently make reference to homes for sale as "listings." A "listing" on an internet site shows information on the home, like the price and number of bedrooms.

Inspection

After you've made an offer on a home, you'll need to schedule an inspection, which costs around $500 – $800, with regards to the market. The inspector will go through every nook and cranny, and review things such as the plumbing, electrical, foundation, walls, heating, and appliances.

Appraisal

When you apply for a mortgage, your lender will need an appraisal of the property you wish to buy. A licensed appraiser will estimate the home's value centered on comparable homes which have sold in your community and an investigation for the property.

Contingencies

Once you place in an offer on a house, you can specify certain problems that must certanly be met ahead of the deal will go through they are called contingencies. You have to ensure you can actually obtain the loan (a financing contingency), that the inspection does not show anything too crazy (inspection contingency), and that the appraised value is close to what you're offering to cover (appraisal contingency). Those are only several common examples; there are numerous other forms of contingencies, that you should consult with your agent.

Offers and Contracts

Once you find the appropriate home, you'll make an offer from the property with the aid of an agent or attorney. If the seller counters your original offer, it is usually simply because they want additional money or a faster timeline for closing the offer, from which point you'll need to negotiate. When submitting an offer, it is smart to add an individual touch by including a cover letter which explains why you want to purchase the home.

Closing Costs

Be prepared to pay plenty of fees whenever you purchase a house. Typically, closing costs will amount to 2-5% associated with purchase price of your home, and therefore doesn't through the down payment. Common fees include excise tax, loan-processing costs and title insurance.

Title Insurance

After all of the negotiations are done while the seller has accepted your offer, you need to receive a property title report within per week. Most mortgage lenders require you to pay title insurance within the closing costs; title insurers search the general public records to make sure the house seller actually had rights to your title and that there aren't any liens in the home (like an unpaid contractor or unpaid taxes).

ABOUT THE AUTHOR

Diego De Giovanni is a real estate expert, an Italian national specifically from Turin. He kicked off his real estate marketing career in the year 1999 starting with local landscape. Years after properly understanding the principles needed to succeed in the local landscape sector of real estate, he began his passionate exploration of the residential market.

Having conquered both local landscape and residential market for 10 years, he began exploring the opportunities in the London market which gave him the opportunity to collaborate with a real estate company specializing in residential trading. Back in Itay, he has helped several real estate companies start, and nurture their businesses to success.

In the meantime he decides to study the American real estate market to better understand it's dynamics and does so through a big in the industry.

His success did not end with the achievement he has made in Italy, helping businesses. He went further to achieve a path to becoming a Mental Coach while specializing in business and assisting them get result.

THE SECRETS OF EFFECTIVE COMMUNICATION

HOW TO MAKE YOUR CONVERSATIONS MORE MEANINGFUL, SPEAK CONFIDENTLY AND STAY IN CONTROL AT WORK, HOME AND IN RELATIONSHIP

DIEGO DE GIOVANNI

BOOK DESCRIPTION

Do you want to change your life by improving your communication?

Are you ready to learn the art of communication?

Do you want to build trust and strengthen your relationship with effective communication?

Do you want to learn how to communicate effectively with coworkers, friends, kids and your partner?

In this book, we'll be taking a look at some of the most significant elements of change that you can introduce to your life if you want to communicate effectively. Everything written in this book is designed with the idea of helping improve your life and make you an effective communicator.

This book will provide you a set of proven techniques which can help you to transform your life by improving your day to day communication. You'll discover:

• Elements of effective communication
• The importance of body language in communication
• How to communicate with strangers?
• How to build friendship?
• Importance of effective communication
• How to make others feel special through communication?

By using this book and the information inside, you can begin the process of positively transforming Does this sound like the kind of treatment that you want to put in place? Then this book will help you do just that.

In this book, you'll find easy step-by-step instructions on how to communicate effectively under the following headings:

• THE ART OF EFFECTIVE COMMUNICATION
• ELEMENTS OF EFFECTIVE COMMUNICATION
• PRINCIPLES OF EFFECTIVE COMMUNICATION

- HOW TO COMMUNICATE BETTER AT THE WORKPLACE
- HOW TO COMMUNICATE BETTER AT HOME
- BUILD TRUST WITH EFFECTIVE COMMUNICATION
- MINDSET FOR EFFECTIVE COMMUNICATION
- DEVELOPING COMMUNICATION SKILLS
- HOW TO COMMUNICATE EFFECTIVELY AT WORK
- WHY EFFECTIVE COMMUNICATION MATTERS IN THE WORKPLACE
- HOW TO COMMUNICATE EFFECTIVELY WITH KIDS
- EFFECTIVE COMMUNICATION IN RELATIONSHIP
- BENEFITS OF EFFECTIVE COMMUNICATION
- COMMON BARRIERS WHICH PREVENT EFFECTIVE COMMUNICATION
- HOW TO OVERCOME COMMUNICATION BARRIERS?
- EFFECTIVE CONFLICT RESOLUTION COMMUNICATION
- TIPS AND TRICKS FOR COMMUNICATION
- HOW TO DEVELOP GOOD COMMUNICATION SKILLS?
- HOW TO BE A CHARISMATIC CONVERSATIONALIST AND INCREASE YOUR SOCIAL CHARISMA
- TECHNIQUES TO MASTER EVERY COMMUNICATION
- APPLYING COMMUNICATION SKILLS WHEN COMMUNICATING WITH STRANGERS
- HOW TO COMMUNICATE WITH PEOPLE TO BUILD FRIENDSHIPS
- MAKE YOUR CONVERSATIONS UNIQUE AND MEMORABLE
- COMMUNICATING WITH DIFFICULT PEOPLE

•USE LAUGHTER TO LIGHTEN THE CONVERSATION

Turn the page of your old life by Buying this book now. Make a step to your new, better future.

INTRODUCTION

The art of communication is essential to have for anyone to succeed in any field. People use their communication skills to convey their thoughts, feelings and emotions to others. Although all of us communicate in our own way but very few of us know how to communicate effectively.

Learning to effectively communicate takes time and practice, but it can easily be done with enough devotion to your new skill.

Effective communication determines your career success, your relationships with your spouse and other family members, your feeling of being appreciated and understood.

If you want to know how to acquire these skills and become a real master of speech, read on.

THE ART OF EFFECTIVE COMMUNICATION

Good communication is the difference between a good and poor leader, a thriving and a boring relationship and an effective professional and an indifferent one.

Since you are living at a time when communication has never been better, all the more that you need to keep up with the changes and the means by constantly and diligently working on your communication skills. As a start, you can keep reading to better understand what and how communication works.

Communication is the act or process of conveying information, thoughts and ideas from one person to another in the form of speech, written words, signals, body language, visuals or behavior.

Great conversations almost always start with small talk. Many people avoid small talk at all cost. Sure, it can sound rather pointless to go on and on about the weather or the traffic. But such small talk serves as a precursor for breaking the ice and paving the way for truly significant conversations.

Maintain an active presence with your body language. Avoid fidgeting or looking over your shoulder like you're already mapping your way out. There should also be no scrolling on your phone. This can come across as plain disrespectful. Maintain comfortable eye contact. Such a posture will keep the conversation going.

What if you initiate small talk and the listener seems blank? Perhaps you're dealing with a conversation rookie who is still getting over social anxiety. Here, you have to speak some more of yourself to prod a response. Let's say you've met in a work seminar and you ask, 'Is this your first time here?' The person answers with a 'no', then awkward silence. You can add something more about yourself. 'Oh, I've been here before, although the speakers are different this year.' The person is then likely to ask about the previous year's speakers. There! You have a conversation going.

When communicating with others, there are three primary steps that occur - thought, encoding and decoding. If you're the sender, it starts from the information that resides in your mind or otherwise known as thoughts. Encoding happens if you decide to send the message to another person through words or other forms. Finally, decoding completes the process as the receiver translates the thoughts into something he or she understands.

Content is one and it refers to the actual words used when sending the message which is also known as language. The second element is context which refers to the way you delivered the message or otherwise referred as paralanguage. This element encompasses other key communication elements such as body language, gestures, eye expression, emotion and tone of voice.

Unfortunately, even though you've been communicating all your life, misunderstanding words and messages is a common occurrence of everyday life. Every person has different ways of interpreting words and context. You may think that you've communicated your ideas clearly but the receiver may not really fully grasp the importance or the full meaning of the message due to numerous communication barriers.

Anything that prevents you from conveying the message clearly and from the receiver understanding it correctly is considered a communication barrier. Barriers can be psychological or physical and the most common you'll probably face often include differences in culture, background, perception, bias, environment, noise and stress. In some instances, the message itself can be a barrier too especially if the focus is on the facts rather than the idea or message being transmitted.

Since most barriers are external and inherent to the receiver, communicating effectively is a tough feat to take on. Even so, it is one endeavor worth your effort. The key is to focus not on yourself but on the person or people you are trying to communicate to. Forget about being defensive, your ego or the need to feel superior if you truly want to be an effective communicator. Only by aspiring and training yourself to overcome communication barriers will you truly unleash the power of effective communication to every aspect of your life.

ELEMENTS OF EFFECTIVE COMMUNICATION

In a world where communication is a vital part of living and interacting, it is imperative to develop the right skills to make the process as effective as possible. If you want to get ahead at work, connect more with people and be a better leader, having good communication skills is your gateway to success.

Whether you're the sender or receiver of the message, there are important factors you need to constantly work on in order to master the art of communicating effectively.

Speech

One of the most obvious forms of communication is speech. This is basically the verbal aspect of the process where words are used to convey the message. When speaking, it is important to keep it short and simple. That is, focus on the important matters and use the right words to deliver your thought as plainly as you can.

Words that come from your mouth may be only 10% of communication but it is just as equally important as other elements. To truly learn the skill, you need to master how to use the right words when interacting with a diverse group of people.

Body Language

This nonverbal form of communication covers body movement, hand gestures, facial expressions, eye contact and posture. These are nonverbal cues that you need to use and take note of if you want to communicate effectively.

When listening to someone talk, pay attention to body language for better insight about the other person's feelings and attitude. You should make eye contact whenever possible or you may nod occasionally to convey agreement. You should also maintain excellent posture and never cross your arms. In other words, match your body's language with your words to avoid confusion on the part of the receiver.

Tone of Voice

Knowing the correct tone to use is critical for effective communication because the right tone can convey the right emotion. Whether you want to be authoritative, friendly, passive or convincing, it's all a matter of injecting the correct tone that will help influence the other person and understand your underlying message more accurately.

Active Listening

Another essential skill you need to master is active listening. When communicating with other people, you're not only a talker but you should also be a good listener. And it's not just about hearing words, filtering it and choosing only what you want to understand.

Active listening is paying attention not just to the words but also to body language and tone.

Also part of active listening is to avoid interruption when the other person is still talking. Wait for your turn and while doing so stay focused on the conversation at hand. Avoid articulating your responses in your mind and more importantly, avoid making judgments. Whether you agree with the person you are communicating with or not, judgment should be reserved and set aside.

Stress Management

With stress in the picture, you or the person you are talking to will see things differently. The way you think, act and respond may be disrupted leading to confusion and misunderstanding. To avoid sending out mixed nonverbal cues and unhealthy negative behaviors, you need to know how to manage stress. For some people, meditating helps while others exercise or go for a run to temper the problem.

There is no one standard formula to managing stress. They key is to find out ways that work for you.

PRINCIPLES OF EFFECTIVE COMMUNICATION

The art of communication is essential to have for anyone to succeed in any field. People use their communication skills to convey their thoughts, feelings and emotions to others. Although all of us communicate in our own way but very few of us know how to communicate effectively. Just like everything has some principles to follow, effective communication is based on five important principles and it is not possible to excel in this skill without considering these principles.

Listening

Listening is very important in the effective communication as those people who are great listeners, are great communicators actually. If you have the ability to convey your thoughts and ideas in an excellent way that everyone understands and appreciates them but your listening skills are poor, your communication will not be effective at all because you will not be able to get the thoughts and ideas of others completely so, you can't respond to them appropriately. This causes frustration for the speaker and the process of communication becomes very difficult.

Proper listening does not only mean that you understand the words or the information being given by the speaker but it also means that you understand the feelings and emotions which the speaker is trying to convey to the listeners.

Therefore, in order to make your listening effective, you have to pay full attention to enhance these skills. As you improve in this area, your listening will automatically get better and this way you make the speaker enjoy the conversation as they realize that you are getting their each and every point.

Effectiveness

When your communication skills are effective, you can develop good understanding with others. People you interact with will understand you, and you will understand them, and this mutual understanding is something that makes the relationships stronger and long-lasting. You won't need to use manipulation or other tactics to win the hearts of others. This will ultimately result in satisfaction with your management and they will trust you more than others.

Perceptual Filters

Sometimes people speak in certain codes and one has to be aware of them in order to pick everything correctly during the conversation. Different people have different perceptual filters that they use in communication to understand others and convey their thoughts or information.

You should pay attention to how you can learn the perceptual filters of certain people you are in interaction with, so that you can communicate with them in better way. This way there won't be any confusion and you will be able to build a healthy relationship with them.

Patience

Patience is much needed in the effective communication because it takes both time and effort to make others understand your ideas and gain the complete information and sometimes failing to do so puts you in frustration and you want to give up on your intention. At that stage, don't forget that you have to win not to lose, so just keep the positive attitude, try to find the right words to communicate your thoughts and you will ultimately succeed.

You might be failing because the words you were using were not passing through the perceptual filters of the listeners and they were not able to understand you properly.

Relationships

What you can achieve with effective communication is stronger relationship with others.

When you learn and start following the principles of effective communication on daily basis at your work place, you are not far away from achieving your goals. All you have to do is take small steps and practice as much as you can and success will be yours

HOW TO COMMUNICATE BETTER AT THE WORKPLACE

Perhaps one of the reasons that effective communication in the workplace is being taken for granted in some workplaces is because some people don't really know what it means. What is effective workplace communication, anyway?

Bosses just send emails to the managers and the managers do the same to the supervisors. The supervisors then just relay important updates to the employees through text messages, Skype chat or some other form of digital communication. In the past, when there was important news to be shared with the workers of a company, the upper management would call for a meeting with the middle management and the middle management would have a meeting with the workers afterward. These days, however, there just isn't time to hold traditional meetings. The speed at which businesses move prevents people from connecting on a personal level, and people have learned to sacrifice face-to-face communication for faster business transactions.

However, effective communication in the workplace is not limited only to the means by which messages are sent.

Being able to communicate better in the workplace is essential for your career. Imagine the stress and failure you'd undergo if you're not able to convey your true thoughts and brilliant ideas. While your colleagues succeed, you're left wallowing in a corner because you can't express your ideas, thoughts, and plans for your company. To assist you in communicating better at your workplace, here are steps you can implement.

Establish Convenient Venues of Communication

As a personnel and part of a team, you have to establish a venue where your colleagues can communicate with you conveniently. You can connect with them online or offline. Having person-to-person communication is, of course, best because you can also interpret any non-verbal language. Let your colleagues know that you're open to communication.

Be Honest and Sincere

You can only become a better communicator if you're honest and sincere. Conveying your message honestly will benefit you too, because you can say what you want without fear because you're honest and sincere. Couple this with diplomacy, though, so that there will be no bad blood between you and your colleagues. You must observe sincerity too, due to the fact that without it, the message you want to convey can fall on deaf ears. Your honesty and sincerity will shine through and your colleagues will trust you more.

Settle Disputes Directly with the Person Concerned

You have to talk to the person concerned first, before anything else. There are many employees who report to higher-ups first, before talking to the person concerned. This is not the proper way to do it. You have to know the other person's side first, and take it from there. Remember to observe honesty, tact, and respect when talking to this person. If he or she shouts, keep calm. If he or she curses, don't curse back. You can't fight fire with fire. Choose the high road instead and you'll end up winning.

Listen More and Talk Less

A great conversationalist listens more and talks less. You can communicate better this way. It's a two-way process that allows you to convey what you want to say. When the person becomes aware that you're not condescending or talking down, he or she will gradually loosen up and listen more to you.

Express Yourself Properly

Be articulate in your language and use brief but exact statements. Tactfulness, of course, is more important than brevity. Whenever you find yourself in a sticky situation, it's better to use more words to be tactful than being brief but rude. Rudeness has no place in good communication. Here are some pointers you can adapt to express yourself properly.

Talk in a normal manner

Don't rush through your words or falter in your speech. Speaking in a normal manner signifies your desire to be heard correctly. Avoid mumbling to yourself.

Maintain the proper distance

This will depend on the person you're talking to. If the individual is a superior, then you can position yourself a comfortable distance away from him or her. If it's a friend, then you can stand closer. Don't let the person misunderstand you just because you've kept an inappropriate distance.

Avoid mannerisms

Focus on the person you're talking to and avoid mannerisms. Don't play with your hair, or bite your fingernails while talking. These actions can be misconstrued negatively.

Listen attentively

Whether you're speaking to a family member or a colleague, you have to listen attentively. What does the individual truly want to say? What's the true meaning of his or her statements?

Show respect

Express yourself to the other person in a respectful manner, and you'll likewise earn the other's respect. You can emphasize a point by speaking calmly and respectfully.

Use simple, understandable language

You have to adjust your language to the level of your receiver. However, you don't have to use highfalutin words to express your ideas. The simpler your language is, the more understandable it is.

HOW TO COMMUNICATE BETTER AT HOME

Now, let's take what we've learned and apply it to the home environment with these simple steps

Keep Communication Lines Open

You can't communicate well if there are no venues open for its fruition. You'll have to allow every member of your family a way to contact you or reach each other. You can use cell phones, emails, tweets, Facebook posts, or snail mail to communicate. Let your family members know where they can reach you promptly. Remember to respond immediately to any form of communication from any member. This way, they'll know that they can keep in touch with you anytime and anywhere, and they'll know they're a priority.

Learn How to Express Yourself Appropriately

Since you know the characteristics of your family members more than anyone else, you should also know how to convey your message properly. If you're talking to a younger person, you can speak as a concerned adult. On the other hand, if you're speaking to another adult, you can talk as an equal so as to avoid sounding condescending.

Strive to speak in a calm manner, even when you're angry, and they'll listen to you.

When you're angry, don't immediately open your mouth. Instead, take time to relax or to take deep breaths first before saying anything. There are three things you can never get back in this world: lost opportunities, time misspent, and ill-spoken words. Sometimes, hurtful words are even more destructive than physical wounds because they leave deep scars that time cannot always heal.

Settle Differences Before the Sun Sets

Allowing differences to go unsettled at the end of the day will oftentimes lead to prolonged misunderstandings. You must do your best to settle misunderstandings within the day. They're your family – your loved ones - and time is short. Who knows what could happen the following day? Too many people only realize the importance of their families after it's too late. Don't be among them. Be a better communicator by expressing yourself promptly and clearly.

Dialogue with Your Family

Don't assume that since they're family, they will understand everything you say or do. You have to spend time with your family. This may be in a leisurely manner or for pure dialogue. You can combine both leisure and dialogue. In fact, this is an ideal venue where you can interact with each other. Whatever the activity is, you must talk to your family; not a meaningless chatter, but a heart-to-heart talk with them. If you haven't spoken to one member of your family in a long time, now is the time to mend your fences and communicate.

Show by Example, Not by Words

You can always say you're a better communicator than anyone else in your family, but you should demonstrate this through your actions and not through your words. How? By talking to them properly. Show them that when you communicate, you pay attention to the person you're talking to. Make direct eye contact with them, and don't multitask during your conversation. Treat them with respect and love. Don't hold shouting bouts with them. Speak clearly, calmly, and honestly and in a tactful manner. You can motivate your family members to join you in your quest to have open communication within your family.

Respect Each Member

When you respect the person you're talking to, he or she will have to show respect to you too. No matter how rude an individual is, he or she will react to your positive action. Don't react to that individual's rudeness by becoming rude yourself. Why should you change your good character based on the negative action of one family member? You have to motivate that person, instead, to follow your lead and in turn show others some respect too.

Be Honest but Diplomatic

Say what you honestly want to say in a diplomatic manner. This is also one way of showing respect. As previously discussed, you can be honest by expressing what you feel about the other person without attacking him or her; especially when that person you're talking to is someone you love.

Pay Attention to Non-Verbal Language

Listen attentively when you talk with your loved ones. Observe the person's non-verbal language. You can understand a person better if you're aware of his or her body language. A number of lonely persons, drug addicts, and persons with suicidal tendencies were saved because of a relative's accurate interpretation of non-verbal cues.

In addition, you can also strengthen a bond when you can have sincere and focused communication with your family members.

Establish a Communication System within the Family

You can create a communication system within your family where there can be a hierarchy of action. Once this system is in place, it has to be implemented diligently. An example is during emergencies; the first person to be contacted – aside from 911– can be the parents, then the older siblings, and then the younger ones.

You can communicate better at home when you follow these effective steps. Your initial action may not be successful, but keep going. Eventually, through your constant effort to communicate better, other family members will catch on too and emulate your example. Soon, not only you, but your whole family will benefit from your diligence and determination.

BUILD TRUST WITH EFFECTIVE COMMUNICATION

Trust is hard to earn these days partly because of rampant bad behavior but also because of poor communication. Even in this day and age when there are more means and methods for communication, people fail to keep up with the changes. Instead of improving communication skills and using it to inspire loyalty and build trust, the means are at times the reasons why the skill deteriorates.

To succeed in today's age of "Me" generation and stiffer competition, you need to be a good communicator.

If not, others who are more assertive will get ahead of you. Key relationships are also hard to come by without effective communication fostering deeper connection and trust. Though communication is largely about conveying information, ideas, thoughts, messages and news, you also have to remember that it is also partly about building trust.

Now you may ask, how do you build trust through communication? Here's how

Understand what matters to others

Whether with your personal, business or work relationships, one of the best ways to build trust is to know what matters to them. When communicating with other people, you need to turn on your perceptiveness meter. When they know you care about what matters to them, trust is a likely by product.

Listen actively and intently

Listening as part of effective communication couldn't be reiterated more. If you want trust, you need to balance be an expert of both sides of the process. Just look how telephones - one of today's primary means of communicating - work. It has part for talking and for listening which tells you exactly what you should. When you're done taking, give the other person the spotlight and while doing so listen actively to build better connection.

Match words with actions

Just like you need to sync body language with words to facilitate effective communication, you also need to match your words with actions if you want to build trust through communication. When words are backed up by actions and people see that you are a person of your word, credibility is established. And as you more likely already know, credibility is a critical element of trust.

Share opinions with an open mind

You may be an expert of communication but no matter how good you are, you should know that there are always people who will not agree with you. When you share your opinion, tell it like it is an opinion and not an idea you are shoving down on other people's throats.

As the saying goes, respect begets respect. If you can respect other people's opinions even if disagreements exist, fostering trust is going to be easy. After all, trust is not based on whether people like you or your opinion. It's about you respecting others and getting the same in return.

Be honest at all times

While there are instances when information cannot be shared, you still need to live by one of life's golden rules - be honest at all times and expect the same thing in return. Regardless of whom you are talking or interacting with, honesty always come a long way. If you're someone who values and hones integrity, you can definitely expect greater trust in every aspect of your life.

MINDSET FOR EFFECTIVE COMMUNICATION

Before we begin our journey into critical conversations the first thing that we need to look at and master is our mindset. What most people don't know, realize or accept is that our mind is the most underused and most understood organ in the human body. With our minds we can accomplish anything that we can possibly imagine as well as limit ourselves to the most basic of tasks and possibilities.

When it comes to mindset it all comes down to what it is that you want and what you are willing to do or not do to achieve it. When looking at mindset, look at it as a coin. On one side we have everything that we want and desire whereas on the other side of the coin we have all of the excuses and issues that prevent us from achieving our goals. For the majority of us however we walk the edge of the coin looking down at the shiny side of our hopes and desires while favoring or listening to the doubts and echoes from the other side.

Your Self Image

The next layer of our mindset can be found in our self-image. The way that we look at ourselves and the way we perceive others looking at us is a major factor in our mindset and the actions that we engage. For instance, if you are someone who is overweight, doesn't speak well, has a disability or just doesn't feel right physically or emotionally your self-image will be affected by this. One the other side of the coin if you are slender, well educated, has a lot of friends and is healthier than ever your self-image will be greater resulting in more positive outcomes and conversations.

Knowing your abilities and limitations

The third level of mindset is our personal knowledge and understanding of our abilities and limitations. To stat this off I want to first say that no one is perfect. However, if you know that you are not perfect and can accept that you have limitations then you have the foundation to build form and grow.

When we know and accept our limitations we can better position ourselves into situations that we feel comfortable and in control. If we feel comfortable and in control we are more likely to be in a better frame of mind to have more intelligent conversations with our inner voices. If however, we find ourselves in situations that we are not comfortable in it is our job to restructure our mindsets to work in a positive way. And we can do this with critical conversations.

You are an island among many

The final component in regards to mindset is one that is seldom talked about or referred to. This is the knowledge that you are an island among many. What this basically means is that you are responsible for you first and foremost. Where many of us fall into the mindset trap is that we think of others first instead of ourselves. Now, I am not saying that you need to be selfish and self-centered. What I am saying is that at the end of the day when all of the kids are asleep, you are lying there in bed wide awake staring at the ceiling letting the events of the day fill your mind just know that you are one with yourself.

The actions that you perform or fail to perform will ultimately affect you in the end. Your kids will one day go off to school, your spouse may divorce you, you may lose or find another job, get a new house, car or win the lottery or eventually die. It is when we find ourselves in these situations we really begin to have these critical conversations with ourselves. Knowing how we plan to handle these conversations when they arrive will ultimately determine their outcomes.

HOW TO COMMUNICATE EFFECTIVELY AT WORK

If there was ever a place where communication skills mattered the most, it is in the workplace. If you can master the ability to communicate effectively with not just your colleagues, but your superiors, managers and all staff levels in every industry, you are in a position of power because you hold one of the most valuable skills an employee can possess.

Even though we live in a digital age where the majority of our work is conducted online, over the phones, emails or even through social media (as a lot of companies tend to do their marketing these days), effective communication skills are still a prized asset that is not going to go away anytime soon. Aside from being able to communicate well to survive in everyday life, there is one other scenario in which effective communication is a crucial skill that you are going to need if you want to succeed – the workplace.

Whether you work in a team or if your profession requires you to interact with customers and clients daily, certain situations can be challenging to handle. Without the right communication skills, it can be even more of a challenge. Imagine trying to persuade a dissatisfied client without being able to properly convey the message that you want. You could just end up putting the client off even more and put yourself at risk of losing their business if they have a hard time understanding what you are trying to say. Do you see how important being able to communicate well is?

How to Improve Communication Skills at the Workplace?

The most successful people who eventually go on to become leaders and managers in the workplace are the ones who can make great impressions on everyone they work with because of how well they communicate. Of course, being able to do the job well does play a part of it as well, but when you can meaningfully and effectively communicate with the people you work with, you are already halfway towards success.

At work, we are required to communicate a lot more than we normally would in our everyday lives. We're communicating with clients, with colleagues, with managers, with bosses, through emails, over the phone and even during meetings and presentations.

Improve Your Body Language

Body language is applicable in the workplace too, perhaps even more so because this is where it really matters. At work, the way you carry yourself and communicate is just as important as how well you get the job done. Remember how our nonverbal cues can speak volumes even when we don't say a word? So, while at work, always adopt confident body language whenever you step into your workplace. Do not slouch, do not fold or cross your arms, do not frown or look sullen. Always be positive, and project a warm and welcoming manner, smile and make eye contact with the people you pass by.

Avoid Over-Communicating

Avoid being long-winded and beating around the bush when you have discussions and conversations at work. You may think you are trying to be as effective as possible by communicating every little detail, even what is seemingly unnecessary, but avoid doing that because there is such a thing as over-communicating. Even in presentations, droning on for too long puts you at risk of losing the attention span of your audience. The best way to communicate effectively is to be brief, concise and only communicate what is necessary and relevant to the situation or discussion at hand.

Seek Feedback

The best way to know if you are effective in what you do, or if what you are doing is working, is to seek feedback honest feedback from your colleagues. Regularly seeking feedback will help you discover what areas you should be working on to improve, and often it is others who can shed better perspective on the things that we may overlook.

Engage with Your Audience

If you are tasked with presenting at a meeting, this is a great way for you to put into practice your effective communication skills. Now, business presentations are not the most riveting topic, and attention spans will drift eventually, so what do effective communicators do? They engage with their audience. Being effective in your communication requires that you can deliver the points you want to say to an audience that is paying attention. During the meeting or presentation, ask questions and encourage your audience to respond and share their points of view.

Watching Your Tone of Voice

At the workplace, you need to always ensure that your tone is professional yet friendly and welcoming at the same time. Sometimes it may be necessary to be assertive to stand firm on a point, but still, try and maintain a professional tone when you do that to avoid coming off as aggressive. Effective communication at work requires that you be able to master being confident, direct, professional yet calm and cooperative at the same time.

Checking Your Grammar

This step is applicable for emails and written communication at the workplace. The most effective communicators are ones who can write flawlessly with no mistakes because they put in the extra effort to check and proofread everything that they type or write before they hit the send button. Check it twice, check it thrice, check it as many times as you need to ensure everything is completely on point before it gets sent. You will impress everyone with your perfect grammar and punctuation, and the ones who read your emails will be able to understand what you are trying to say just as if you were standing there in front of them talking to them.

Speaking with Clarity

Good communication means being able to be easily understood by everyone you speak to. Practice being able to put forth the messages that you want to say is as few and concise words as possible, this will help you speak with clarity because you already know exactly what needs to be said. Preparing your talking points ahead of time is another great way to boost speech clarity and keep the conversation fillers to a minimum. It also helps avoid excessive and unnecessary talking about irrelevant points, because you want your receiver to be clear about the message, not walk away from the discussion still feeling more confused about it.

Practice Friendliness

Would you enjoy speaking to someone who is unfriendly and stand-offish at the office? The obvious answer would be no. Nobody would want to engage in a conversation because they would be put off by the person's very demeanor even before they have said a word. To become an effective communicator at work, you need to start adopting a friendly and approachable persona which will encourage your co-workers to want to approach you and have a conversation with you. A friendly approach is even more important when you are having a face-to-face discussion, especially if you are in a managerial position because your colleagues aren't going to want to open up to you if they feel intimidated even before the discussion has properly begun.

Be Confident

Being confident is an important part of becoming an effective communicator overall. When you interact with others around you at the workplace, the moment you show you are confident you will find it much easier to hold effective conversations with your colleagues and team members that will result in things getting done. Why? Because they are drawn towards your confident approach. Confident people are not thwarted by challenges, they rise to meet them, and this is what people at work want to follow.

Say No to Distractions

Meeting rooms exist in the workplace for a reason, and its time to make full use of them. The best way to have a meaningful conversation with the people you work with is to keep the distractions to a minimum. In an environment like work where so many people are working in close proximity with one another, phones can be constantly ringing off the hook, people will be on the move walking up and down, and several conversations could be going on at once. Not exactly the most conducive environment to hold a discussion, much less an effective conversation.

Keep the distractions to a minimum, go into a meeting room and close the door, put the phones away and then when both parties are ready, begin your conversation.

Keep Your Points Consistent

To be able to deliver messages effectively means you need to be able to remain on point and consistent with what you are saying. It helps if you stick to the facts and the focus of the discussion at hand, write down and prepare your talking points before you hold the conversation. Your points should flow smoothly, and nothing should contradict each other because you could end up confusing the receiver of your message and they become unsure about what it is you are trying to say. Your key points of your message are also at risk of being lost when you contradict yourself far too much. Plan and prepare ahead, make some notes and have them ready if you need to refer to them to help you stay on course. This is how you practice becoming a more effective communicator.

Remain as Transparent as Possible

There is nothing that is disliked more at the workplace than a lack of transparency. Never try to hide information, or leave out bits and pieces of information when working with your colleagues on a project or working in a team. It makes it difficult for everyone involved to communicate well if they don't have all the necessary information on hand to work with.

Why effective communication matters in the workplace

Effective Communication Forms and Maintains Relationships and Rapport

At the workplace, it is important to maintain positive and amicable relationships with your co-workers. You are going to spend most your day working together with them, and without the proper communication skills on hand, it can be difficult to build and construct productive relationships with the ones you work with.

Effective Communication Promotes Innovation

Innovation at the workplace increases when its employees are comfortable and confident enough to openly communicate their ideas and work well with one another. When employees are not able to communicate their exact thoughts and ideas, or if they don't feel confident enough to do so, the chances of good ideas ever being implemented in the workplace become slim to none.

Effective Communication Builds Better Teamwork

When effective communication flows freely in the workplace, it is easier to build teams which are productive and cohesive, who work well together to get things done. When employees within a team can communicate and get along well with one another, the staff morale is given a boost because they feel confident in what they are during. When the management communicates the company's mission and vision effectively, the employees will turn feel more secure in their roles and be able to perform better as a result. Work ethics are also improved when internal communication within a company is excellent because the staff fully understand what common goal it is that they are working towards.

Effective Communication Can Boost the Growth of the Company

A company relies on effective marketing to generate business and sales. Marketing is about delivering strong messages across to the clients, making sure that those messages hit the target right where they are supposed to. How is this done? By relying on effective communication.

Communication, especially in the marketing role, is crucial because, without the great marketing collateral, good communication internally and externally becomes a struggle for the company. When the company starts to struggle, it is only a matter of time before it folds because it is not able to work to overcome those barriers.

Effective Communication Helps Promote Transparency

Transparency at the workplace is important to help build trust in the brand. This trust must be gained both internally among the employees, and externally among the clients. Transparency and effective communication go hand-in-hand because when it comes time for tough decisions to be made, the company leaders will have a much easier time explaining why to their employees if they practice effective communication.

Effective Communication Will Boost Customer Service

If you are going to provide top-notch service to your clients, you are going to need to be able to understand what they want. Exactly what they want. If you don't, there is no way you are going to be able to meet their needs or even go the extra mile to deliver the best service you possibly can. No matter what you may be selling, your relationship with your clients relies heavily on your ability to be able to communicate effectively, because you need to be able to convince them why they should go along with your business instead of your competitors.

HOW TO COMMUNICATE EFFECTIVELY WITH KIDS

To start you on your journey in critical communications we are going to talk about kids. For most of us kids aren't really looked upon as people who we have deep and meaningful conversations with. In fact, most people will look at children as needing to be educated and told what to do rather than sit down with them and have a meaningful conversation.

Yes, it is true that there are topics and subject depending on the age rage of the child you may not be able to talk to them about or if you did they may not have the mental or emotional maturity to understand and react to the conversation but as a whole child are pretty smart, are extremely creative and uninfluenced by the adult baggage we carry with us.

What is their age?

When adjusting your mindset, you need to look at the age of the child. In today's day and age, it seems that children are growing up and turning into adults at five and six years of age but the truth is that they are still children and they need to be addressed as children.

Understanding of the world

What is their understanding of the world? With the introduction of the Internet and its wide spread acceptance and use in our day to day lives it is getting to be harder and harder to shield our children from these things as we once did. In today's world our children can find out pretty much anything that they want to know with a simple Google search.

As such it is critical that we understand their understanding of the world. With so much misinformation and conflicting information it is easy for them to become confused and form their own opinion on the world. When communication with children it is very important that you listen to them, watch what they do and educate yourself on their world so that it is much easier for you to communicate with them in theirs.

Educate yourself and them

In the education process of communication with children you as the parent need to educate yourself to their world. One of the most important aspect of this education will be their language. Throughout time starting back in the 1960's or so children began to come up with phrases, terms and their own universal language that makes perfect sense to them but is a foreign tongue to the rest of us.

When we were growing up the word "Cool" meant one thing and ten years later the word "Bad" means just the opposite. It is the constant shifting of these words, meanings and global understanding that makes communication so difficult.

You can begin to understand the context to their conversations and begin to pull our red flags that as a parent you will want to be aware of. From there you will want to start observing and monitoring their body language and communications. Now, I am not saying to go out there and spy on your kids or install Nanny Software on your kids computers but I am saying if you want to learn how to communicate with your kids or children in general it is important that you educate yourself with the same material that they are educating themselves with.

Lead by example

When it comes to communication with children words might not be the best way to get your point and meaning across. Again, depending on the age and emotional maturity of those you are talking to these actions may not fit but if you use actions over words then you may have a better communication medium to turn to.

When dealing with children not all children will do what you want them to do. In fact, the odds are they will probably do the opposite. So, what are you to do in order to get them to change their mindset to reflect yours?

The first thought would be to sit them down and talk to them like an adult. Again, they are not adults and trying to move them up into your position as an adult and expect them to understand is harder and less effective than other options. The next thought or option that many will turn to is punishment. To start with people will send their kids to their rooms, take away privileges. On the surface this seems like a good way to gain control and teach someone a lesson when in fact it just shuts down the lines of communication which in turn pushes people away from each other.

The final action that people will use for communication is physical and emotional abuse or intimidation. This is a tactic that should never be used and in fact destroys all lines of communication since those being abused will just shut down and do whatever it takes to keep things away from their abuser out of fear.

Be Patient

When it comes to communicating with children it is important that you be patient. You need to understand and adjust your mindset, education and actions according to each specific situation. Remembering and understanding this will go a long way to keeping the line of communication open.

Keeping the lines of communication open

And finally the best way to communicate with a child and anyone for that matter is to create a secure and welcoming environment. If we let children know that we are always there to talk, have proven that they can talk to us on a wide range of subject and that they won't get physically or emotionally abused then communication becomes that much easier.

EFFECTIVE COMMUNICATION IN RELATIONSHIP

Divorce across the world is rapidly becoming a multi-billion-dollar business. In fact, ins the United States divorce is almost as popular and even as widely celebrated as weddings. When a couple gets married the entire world looks bright and filled with possibilities. Typically, those who get married in their early twenties, are just getting out of school, finding bright promising new jobs and in their minds nothing can go wrong. Unfortunately, just like with all things in life something will always go wrong somewhere along the way. And how you and your partner deal with these situations will ultimately determine the health and well-being of this marriage.

The Lines of Communication

When entering into a lifelong partnership with another individual there has to be a specific bond that transcends everything else. This is the mindset layer of communications. When we get married it is considered to be a union of both body and soul. At the end what is yours is mine and what's mine is yours. This needs to be the foundation of a marriage if it is going to work.

As such the lines of communication are critical in expressing this understanding. Once the lines of communication are broken down there is little or no chance to repair them.

Emotional health

It is important that each party feel physically and emotionally safe. They need to know that if an issue needs to be discussed that it can be discussed and worked on. If at any time the emotional health of your partner is weakened it will take some time to recover if at all.

This is why it is important to build trust in your relationship before even entering into marriage. I am talking about a deeper trust that can only be found in a marriage.

Keeping Secrets

When it comes to keeping secrets there are two sides to the coin. There is the side of the coin where you shouldn't keep secrets from your partner and the other side where you shouldn't be spreading secrets to others.

When we keep secrets form our partners we are doing much more damage than we would if we just kept the lines of communication open. If for example, we tell our spouse that we don't like their cooking then we may make them feel bad for a short period of time. If we don't tell them that we don't like their cooking we may end up eating crap meals that they believe we enjoy.

Keeping secrets from others

When we are in relationships with others there will be many times that things are said and done that we feel are harmless and could be told to others when in reality they are very embarrassing and could either cause emotional or other harm. This is where our education about the emotional health of others comes into play.

For example, if your spouse tells you a secret about a co-worker or even just a story about something that happened at work and you happen to mention it to someone else who in turn tells someone else and this information gets back to the person the story was about then this puts your spouse in an awkward position where trust has been broken.

When your spouse gets home that night they may be upset at you for telling a story that was told to you in confidence. Now, it may not have been stated outright that this information was confidential or that you shouldn't tell another about it, but rather it was implied due to the bonds of your relationship.

This is where communication and understanding of your unspoken language is critical. If the lines of communication are broken or message and meanings are not spoken plain as day situations like these will occur on a regular basis.

Developing rules of behavior

When in a relationship it is vital that you develop rules of behavior and have a clear understanding of these rules and their consequences if they are broken. In the above example it would be a good rule to state that anything that is talked about in the bedroom or talked about alone should never be talked about in public. If this rule is broken both parties should understand that unforeseen consequences may occur.

Joking around isn't a joke

When working on the emotional health of your partner joking around may do more damage than intended. As adults we have very little time for fun and enjoyment. Our days are typically filled with dealing with the kids, working a long job, paying bills and other non-exciting activities.

When we do find time to let our hair down and have fun jokes, funny stories and pranks may occur. When it comes to your spouse however you may want to think twice and even three times before pulling that prank or saying the punchline. This is why you need to setup boundaries and guidelines that you can follow so these jokes don't turn into arguments.

Have nightly or weekly meetings

When it comes to communication having a meeting might sound stupid or embarrassing. The truth is however when you setup a time to have a family meeting or if you are just a couple without kids, a date night meeting where a safe environment is created you can more easily get problems and thoughts off your chest and resolved before they grow and pile on.

Just communicate

In conclusion many people believe that the reasons for divorce in this country is the lack of money. This is not the reason. The reason for divorce is the lack of communication or waiting too long to start communicating. The sooner you start and the less concern you have on the feelings of others the more likely you can fix problems before they occur.

BENEFITS OF EFFECTIVE COMMUNICATION

Communication, quite simply, is defined as the exchanging of information that we do amongst ourselves and other individuals.

If you live in this world, you need to relate to others around you. Nobody can survive without having their needs met, and to have our needs met, whether we like it or not, requires the help of other individuals to do so. And therefore, we need to rely on communication to get by.

Communication is a skill that many don't think twice about, but it is one of the most important skills you could have at your disposal. If you want to know what it is like not to be able to communicate or be understood, just picture a time when you have gone to a foreign country where you do not speak the local language.

Everything suddenly becomes more difficult, doesn't it? You struggle to understand and to make yourself understood, and even simple forms of communication like asking for directions seems like an impossible task. Communication, both verbal and nonverbal, matters. It matters because it helps us relate and collaborate with the people living in the world with us.

Helps Express Ideas & Pass Information

Think of all the greatest inventions that we have in our lives today. All of those came to fruition because the inventors were able to communicate their brilliant ideas to the rest of the world. Effective communication is the reason people can facilitate the process of information and knowledge sharing so seamlessly. Without it, a lot of our ideas, thoughts, and points of view would just be trapped inside our head, and we would not know what to do about it. If you can effectively master the art of communication and make it easy for people to understand, your chances of conveying the information without the danger of being completely misinterpreted will increase that much more.

Messages are Conveyed Clearly

The receiver understands you and your message. There will be fewer misunderstandings because people in your workplace and at home will not misconstrue your words. Your intended meaning is conveyed.

Increased Frequency of Conflicts

Many people don't mean what they say and do. They're just unfamiliar with the proper way of relaying their thoughts, ideas, and emotions. If a person doesn't take time to hone his communication skills, he'll most likely get sucked into conflicts, which could have been easily avoided. Many arguments are actually unnecessary because they just stemmed from the wrong tone of voice or wrong choice of words. Further, lack of eye contact and inappropriate gestures can also turn a peaceful conversation into an exchange of horrible words.

One of the main elements of good communication is respect between two conversing sides. If respect is not shown, then ill reactions will certainly ensue. Whether you're talking with a family member, friend, or a colleague, it's always necessary to communicate with respect. Decrease the frequency of conflicts and avoid getting into a heated argument with anyone by learning how to use words and gestures well.

Better Relationships

Your relationships will improve because you can express yourself well. Your family and coworkers will surely appreciate an honest and sincere person around them. When you know how to express yourself honestly without inflicting harm, then your relationships will significantly improve.

Improved Communication Skills

You're able to correctly say what you want to say and in a diplomatic manner. You can express your thoughts honestly but tactfully. You know how to interpret body language and relate it to what the other person is saying. You'll learn how to maintain a good conversation without batting an eyelash.

Less Stress

When you know that you're able to express yourself freely without hurting someone unintentionally, you'll be less stressed and less anxious. The fear of being unable to communicate properly and saying the right things are major sources of stress and anxiety. This can cause you to always be on your toes, wary of instances that would force you to communicate with other people.

A Healthier Life

Do you know that stress is the root cause of a number of diseases such as hypertension, hyperacidity, and cardiac disease? In Virginia, numerous studies have proven this fact already. Less stress and anxiety, in turn, will lead to a healthier life.

A More Successful and Happy Life

When your relationships at home and in your workplace are improved due to your improved communication skills, your endeavors are more likely to succeed as well. Everyone will strive to cooperate with you to achieve your goals. This will allow you to lead a happier life.

These are the benefits you can attain when you communicate better. Communication serves a crucial part of your daily life and you have to strive to develop it if you want to go through life like a winner.

Reduces Misunderstanding

We all know what happens when information is misunderstood or taken out of context. Heated arguments arise, fights happen, and sometimes relationships get severed because misunderstood information causes hurt feelings or hit a sore spot with someone. That is another major reason why effective communication is such a vital skill to possess. You exist in this world; you need to be able to express your messages clearly and to the point to minimize the chances that what you are going to say is going to cause problems for yourself and the people that you are speaking to.

Effective Communication Increases Your Confidence

That's because they're able to communicate well. When you can communicate effectively, your self-esteem and confidence level rise because you do not doubt at all that you can express and tell people exactly what you want them to know. When you can communicate well, you find that you are no longer shy and awkward when it comes time for you to speak, because you know exactly what to do and how to handle the situation.

Effective Communication Will Help You Go Far

If you want to be successful at everything you do in life, you need to confidently be able to communicate effectively, because this is how you are going to set yourself apart from the rest. Do you notice how the most successful people in the world are the ones who can communicate effortlessly?

COMMON BARRIERS WHICH PREVENT EFFECTIVE COMMUNICATION

Messages may not come across or be received in the way that we intended, which is why it is important to understand the causes of communication barriers and what can be done to overcome them.

During the communication process, there are sometimes barriers which tend to come up that can result in poor communication. These are known as communication barriers, and these are the reasons your messages become misunderstood, taken out of context or even distorted. To overcome these communication barriers, you must first understand what they are.

Here's a list of some common communication barriers which occur frequently

Language Differences

Different languages come with different accents, and sometimes, difficulty understanding a person's accent can also be a communication barrier. Perhaps they may be pronouncing certain words differently, or the way their sentences run together may be difficult to understand because of a thick accent for example.

Making Assumptions

A common communication barrier, this frequently occurs when someone decides to reach a decision or course of action without fully listening to all the information at hand. Making assumptions can lead to complications because when you are not well informed, you run the risk of making more mistakes than you should.

Lack of Attention

Not paying full attention is considered a communication barrier. Sometimes, our mind tends to wander or drift when someone else is talking. Or we may be the ones who are doing the talking, but we run the risk of losing the other person's interest because the topic doesn't rivet them enough. When attention starts to drift, it can be easy to miss crucial points in the message.

Current Emotional State

There may be times when it isn't necessarily the best time to bring up a certain subject or topic of discussion. Emotions such as sadness, anger, nervousness, distraction or frustration can hamper the way messages are communicated or received. If someone is not in the right frame of mind or state to pay full attention to what you have to say, they may not be able to process that message appropriately.

A Lack of Confidence

Lacking confidence is also viewed as a communication barrier. When a speaker lacks the necessary confidence needed, they become shy and find it difficult to assert themselves properly, making it difficult to convey messages or make their opinions known. Lacking confidence can result in a lot of awkward pauses, stammering, and stuttering, which could garble the messages and prevent them from being communicated effectively.

Rushing Through the Message

Never convey messages in a rushed or hasty manner. Doing this puts you at risk of missing out crucial information that needs to be communicated, and your listener could miss out on possible information too because they're unable to keep up with what you may be saying. Rushing through messages is never a good idea unless you have the time to spare for a proper discussion, don't do it.

Talking Unnecessarily

Effective communication skills are a powerful tool that anyone can use to achieve success in both personal and professional life. Most common obstacle in communication many people face is unnecessary talk as no one likes to have conversation with the person who talks excessively and irrelevantly.

In order to overcome this obstacle, you have to analyze your thoughts in your mind before you share with others so that you can talk to the point and everyone understands you easily.

Being Prejudiced

A very harmful element that not only breaks the team spirit but also destroys the environment of healthy competition is Prejudice. When you are prejudiced, you are not willing to pay attention to what is being said and you don't understand it at all.

In order to overcome this obstacle in communication, you have to treat the speaker respectfully and value their opinion and thoughts about whatever they are speaking, regardless of negative things associated with them. Try to bring change in your thinking with positive mindset that their knowledge is the most important thing to you and nothing else.

Distractions

There are four kinds of distractions that may arise as an obstacle in communication and those are mental, physical, auditory and visual distractions. One has to be aware of all of such distractions so the process of communication is not hindered and everything is done smoothly.

Thinking Others Are Imitating You

It's true that some people don't use their mind as much as they should and copy other's ideas and thoughts in their opinions. But it's not necessary that it happens everywhere.

You have to keep your thinking positive and try to learn one important thing that others are not stealing your thoughts but they are sharing their own unique beliefs and values. It is also possible that their suggestions might show a way out of the situations you never got a chance to handle before.

Lack of Confidence

When you can't understand the words or sentences of the speaker correctly at any stage, you are not able to grasp the idea completely and this thing will be a big obstacle for you in communication. You might be afraid that it is not appropriate to tell the speaker that you did not get their point because it can be a bad impression in your perspective but this is not the case at all.

You can feel free to let them know what you are not clear about and they will be happy to clarify their words for your better understanding. They will take it positively and appreciate that you are taking deep interest in whatever is being said.

Improper Way of Interruption

You leave a bad impression on others when you interrupt the speaker with wrong body language or words and this can be a big obstacle in effective communication.

In order to overcome this barrier, you must listen with patience and wait for some pause. When you get a chance, use a decent body language like raising your arm, saying sorry for the interruption and putting your query in front of them very politely.

Absence of Mind

Trying to fake the attention is what many people do when they are not taking interest in the conversation. Although they are having the proper eye contact with the speaker but their mind is diverted to something else. This thing not only creates an obstacle in communication but also shows disrespectful attitude of the listener towards the speaker.

Try to focus your attention at the speaker with the

thought that he or she has got some important knowledge and ideas that you really need to know about. You can keep a notebook with you and write down important points of the conversation. This practice will help you improve your attention span and focus, prevent your mind from getting diverted. This way you won't need to fake your attention during the conversation.

Emotions

Getting emotional during the conversation hinders the communication and one can't understand the speaker properly because during the emotions of anger or sadness our senses can't function at the required level and we are not able to stay focused at the speaker's words.

Noisy Environment

Noise is one of the most common environmental barriers in communication. When there is noisy environment, nothing can be understood during the conversation and it's a waste of time for everyone. The best thing to do is to hold the conversation as far away from the noisy place as possible.

Other options are trying to reduce the noise by switching off the appliances that are creating the noise and talking to people or kids causing the noise that they should choose some other place for their activity.

Fear Factor

One very important factor that does not let you have effective communication is fear. When you have fear of something in your mind, you can't stay engaged in the conversation. You have to defeat that fear by one way or the other, so that you can keep yourself calm. In order to do this, you should take deep breadths and try to make your mind free from all the negative thoughts coming from outside.

HOW TO OVERCOME
COMMUNICATION BARRIERS

Now that you know the type of barriers which can occur that prevent effective communication from happening, here comes the next question. How do we overcome these barriers?

Take Steps to Clarify

To help improve the effectiveness of your message going across, spend sometimes clarifying the message that you want to communicate before you communicate it. If it helps, write down what you want to say, it makes it easier to assess your message when you see it written down in front of you. To help you determine if your message is clear enough, ask yourself is the objective of the message clear, ask yourself if you are getting all the important information across, and analyze which aspect of the message could be misunderstood and what can you do to prevent that from happening.

Communicate with Your Receiver in Mind

Messages sometimes need to be adjusted and tweaked a little bit depending on whom you are talking to. Remember that people tend to process information differently? You wouldn't necessarily communicate a certain message to your boss the same way that you would to your colleague or a friend. The way you talk and your approach would be completely different. When preparing to communicate, to ensure that your message is the most effective, you need to structure and prepare it according to who is going to receive the message. Making it easier to understand for the receiver improves your chances of that message being communicated effectively.

Keep the Language and Tone in Mind

When attempting to communicate your messages, you – as the communicator – need to ensure that you frame those messages in a clear, easy to understand language. You also need to be aware of the tone you use to deliver that message. Ideally, it should be in a manner that will not risk offending or injuring the feelings of the receiver. The language used to deliver those messages should also be kept brief, concise and to the point, avoid using unnecessary jargon or technical terms where possible because those could just overcomplicate things.

Keep Your Messages Consistent

When communicating, you need to take extra measures to ensure that your messages remain consistent and your points don't contradict each other. What you are trying to convey should be consistent and with a clear focus in mind, so as not to confuse your recipient. When communicating at work, ensure that your messages are clearly in line with company's objectives, mission, and policies, so your colleagues or employees are clear on what needs to be done.

Listening Effectively

Being able to listen effectively is also part of the effective communication process. Both the communicator and the receiver must be able to listen effectively to one another while each is expressing their points of view. Relevant and important information is in danger of being missed if you are not able to listen well to what the communicator is trying to say to you. And in the case of the communicator, they would also need to be able to listen to the feedback that they are receiving if they hope to improve their communication skills moving forward.

Minimize Distraction

To avoid your messages being lost in translation, finding a good place where you can conduct a discussion is going to be your best bet. The less the distraction, the higher the chances of improved concentration and focus when a discussion is taking place, thereby improving effective communication.

Using the Right Word Selection

Word selection is important in determining how effective your messages come across. Words are the source of facilitating effective communication, and careless or improper use of words are usually the reason for poor communication. To improve the effectiveness of your communication, start by carefully considering the types of words used in delivering your message. Minimize the use of jargons, slangs and overly technical terms which may not necessarily be understood by your receiver.

Avoid Inflicting an Air of Superiority

Whether you are discussing with your friends or your co-workers, even if you feel that you are well versed and more knowledgeable about the subject at hand, do not inflict an air of superiority when you are having a discussion. Be relatable and talk to your receiver like an equal, because this helps them be more receptive and attentive to the things you have to say.

Using Visuals

This step is more appropriate for meetings or presentations conducted at work. Instead of droning on and on, at risk of losing the attention of your audience, try including some message-related visuals into your presentation. Not only will this help break the monotony, but you will continue to hold the attention of your audience, improving the chances of your message getting across.

Communication barriers will happen from time to time, whether we like it or not. Whether in everyday life or the workplace, effective communication makes a difference in the way you convey yourself and how easily you are understood by others around you. The way it works is simple – the easier you are to understand, the better your chances of achieving success in whatever task you are undertaking at the moment.

The best thing to do in this instance to prevent the message from being misunderstood or distorted is to be aware of the situation in which you are holding your communication session, and you your best to minimize the efforts wherever possible. Effective communication is possible, once you have a better understanding of what you can do to encourage it.

EFFECTIVE CONFLICT RESOLUTION COMMUNICATION

Leadership and conflict go hand-in-hand. However, the clinching factor here is how you deal with the conflict. There are plenty of areas in our interpersonal and work life where we deal with conflicts on a daily basis. Think of promotions, salary disputes, personal differences, low appreciation, and other issues. Each time there's a conflict in your business or workplace, you don't have to go running to find another job or business. Instead, be proactive, confront the issue, and remember to avoid personalizing it. Here are a few ways to deal with conflict like a pro.

Try to identify a few common grounds

Even in the most intense conflicts or major differences, there will be something in common with the other party. If nothing else, you both can agree that there is a problem that needs to be resolved. Identify something that you both agree upon, and take off from there. For instance, if you feel like the other person is constantly overpowering you, you both have clear problems there.

Split responsibilities on how each one can tackle their side of the issues to mutually arrive at a solution for the conflict. Say something like "I am sure you are as eager to resolve this as I am. Let us find some solutions we both can agree on to move ahead." You aren't blaming the other person. Rather than making it a battle or competition, you are focusing on arriving at a solution as a team or in collaboration.

If you've made a mistake, promptly offer an apology instead of trying to underplay it. Express regret and accept your mistakes. This doesn't imply you are solely responsible for the problem. It just means that you are accepting your share of the blame to encourage others to follow suit. For instance, "I apologize for uttering those hurtful words. I was angry and upset with what you did.

Tips for giving negative feedback or criticism

While the sandwich method (juxtaposing a negative feedback or criticism between two compliments or positive statements) can be wonderful when it comes to offering feedback or criticism in personal relationships, it may not be very effective in professional scenarios. It may give the worker or employee a false sense of accomplishment, instead of the constructive reality check. If they receive two positive statements, they are likelier to believe they are performing well on the whole. They will most likely take back the compliment rather than criticism, thus preventing further action when it comes to working on their limitations.

What is the work about? Employ constructive criticism that will help identify areas of improvement using a more well-rounded approach. Instead of simply criticizing the person, follow up the critique with a solution. Managers and leaders who offer solutions gain more respect and following if they back-up their criticism with relevant and valuable solutions.

Let us say an employee is constantly writing reports that are filled with grammatical errors. Rather than telling them that it is an issue and they shouldn't do it, explain the ramifications of the problem, followed by an actionable takeaway or solution. You can mention something such as "Though your research and content is fabulous, the grammatical mistakes are pointlessly ruining your reports." Or "If you work on your grammar and sentence construction, you'll create awesome reports." Set timelines and come up with a plan of action to help them work on their weaknesses. Simply telling someone to stop doing something doesn't make you an effective communicator.

This work in our personal life too! When you want someone to change something about them, offer them solutions and a plan of action. Mention the implications of continuing with it and how resolving/overcoming the limitation can better their lives. Honesty is important but it shouldn't border on being painfully blunt. Even though you aren't using the sandwich technique, you still have to keep it positive, polite, and encouraging if you want to get the other person to act on it.

Again, let us take the above example of an employee making too many grammatical errors in their reports. A personal attack in this scenario would be labeling them lazy, sloppy, careless, laidback, irresponsible, incapable, and so on. You are calling out the person instead of the main issue. Yes, they may be all of this. However, you won't get them to listen to you if you launch into a personal attack rampage.

Instead, call out the issue by installing faith in the person and letting them know that you believe "they are capable but just need to be more mindful while drafting their reports." Tell them that you know they are capable of fixing this issue and that it is no big deal for them. Let them know politely yet firmly that the issue needs to be addressed or rectified immediately because you want them to accomplish what you believe they are fully capable of accomplishing. Contrast this with calling out their laziness and inadequacy.

Personal attacks make people instinctively defensive. It shifts focus from the real problem and creates a psychological battle between two people who, more or less, want the same thing. The dynamics change when you make personal attacks, and it worsens the issue instead of rectifying it. Don't divert attention from the real issue by making the recipient of the feedback more defensive.

A person is less likely to be defensive about their actions if they are given an opportunity to rate their own performance.

Also, be specific in giving feedback. Compliments and criticism both should be specific. Avoid talking in vague and generalized terms. Instead, address a specific issue.

Taking the above example, instead of telling the employee that their report was written "ineffectively" (which can imply anything from the writing style to research to grammatical errors to vocabulary), be specific and mention that "their grammar and sentence construction needs work in an otherwise put together report."

Being specific will help the other person identify the exact problem, thus, increasing your chances of getting him/her to take action in the right direction. While offering feedback, refer to specific instances and offer examples. For instance, if you are pulling up an employee for bad behavior, mention specific instances of his/her bad behavior.

Avoid acting on impulse or saying something you'll end up regretting later in a conflict-prone situation. Take time to think through your actions before responding. Mentally, go over the consequences of different actions instead of responding in a harsh and impulsive manner. If you think you need more clarification or a closer examination of facts, take time to seek it before responding. Instant reactions often border on the negative since our emotions are at the peak. Taking time off to analyze the situation more objectively gives us the opportunity to neutralize our emotions a bit.

Again, how to determine if conflict resolution should be kept private or enter the public arena? If the misunderstanding, miscommunication, or conflict happened in the private arena (mail, phone call, or person to person), restrict its resolution within the personal arena as well. However, if the conflict occurred in a public domain or publically, then deal with it publically. Irrespective of where it is brought out, aim to resolve the issues instead of letting it snowball into something bigger.

Build an opening for effective communication so everyone can express themselves or have their say. You can start by mentioning that there is a conflict or it has occurred. Later, add that everyone will be given an opportunity to have their say in the matter. Then, step back and allow people to have their say without any interruptions, judgmental statements, and emotional outbursts. Make it clear at the onset that everyone will be given an opportunity to air their views. This makes people open up, drop their guard, and feel heard.

Repeat your understanding of the issue. This is a part of active listening skills but deserves a special mention in conflict resolution. When there's a conflict, obviously, everyone perceives issues differently. Restate your understanding of the issue by saying something like "If I heard you correctly, I understand that you are not happy about the way things are shaping up with this project due to (reason for conflict)." It is important to make the other person feel heard. It not just confirms your understanding of the situation but also gives the other person an opportunity to correct you in case you've misinterpreted or misunderstood their words.

Use more "I" and less "You" statements during conflict resolution. By framing emotions, thoughts, and feelings around yourself, you accept responsibility for how you feel instead of blaming the other person. This prevents them from becoming defensive and adding to the conflict. "I' statements focus more on facts and resolution, while "you" statements are more emotionally laden. For instance, "You knew how important the client presentation was. Why were you still late for it?" Try framing the same by accepting responsibility for your own reactions. "I felt really upset and frustrated that we couldn't begin our client meeting on time." Now, instead of blaming the person, you are sticking to facts that led you to feel upset.

Let us look at some statements. Instead of saying, "Xyz never consults me or includes me in design-related decisions ever," try saying "I feel upset when I am unaware of the design-related decisions that affect my work until the decisions are already made" or "I find it tough to do the best work possible when I come to know about modifications needed after I've already given it a lot of time and effort." There can be a huge leap in your conflict resolution skills once you accept ownership of your feelings instead of focusing on other's faults and putting them in a defensive mode.

In the end, it is always a good practice to end a conflict by following up in an appropriate manner. Begin by restating the resolution after thanking the person for their involvement in resolving the issue and ensuring open communication. Tell them that you'll be around if they have any issues in the future. This helps to offer a logical closure to the conflict and ensures everyone accepts where you've all arrived.

Where conflicts are concerned (especially workplace conflicts), people often find someone to blame instead of going to the root cause of the matter. Focus on setting the process right instead of making this about a person or group of people. Ask yourself things such as "Did the person have all the relevant information to perform their task correctly? Was there an error in communication that led to the conflict? Was there contextual loss when information or knowledge shared hands?" Focusing on the issue allows you to prevent such conflicts from occurring in the future. It will also give people the confidence that you've got their back when things aren't hunky-dory, something that inspires greater faith and loyalty.

Receiving negative feedback effectively

Again, if you are on the other side of the feedback, avoid taking it personally. Understand that it doesn't speak about your capability or limitations as a person. Distance yourself from the issue or situation. Also, criticism or negative feedback isn't as bad as you think. It is only propelling your growth and taking you in the right direction. Depersonalize the criticism, and instead, focus on growth and development.

Instead, drop their guard by appealing to their rational or logical side. Admit you could be wrong, and that you want to be corrected if you are wrong. Then, go about examining the facts together to prove the other person wrong without making it obvious to them.

While responding to criticism, you can say something such as "I would really like to work on this and do everything I can to change it or find a way ahead." It will make you instantly endearing to the other person. Even something such as "Yes, I have noticed this issue myself. Can we work on a plan of action to help me overcome it?" You are accepting the issue instead of getting defensive. This immediately softens the other person's stand that will be likelier to work with a solution-oriented approach ahead.

Own up to your actions if you know you've goofed up. Accept accountability and responsibility for your actions instead of making excuses, which only ends up strengthening the other person's attacks. Owning your actions shows the other person that you are ready to work towards a solution. When you express thankfulness for the feedback, you are invariably leading yourself towards growth and development.

Avoid fighting facts. Our first instinctive reaction, when faced with facts, is to battle with reality and create our own version about our circumstances (which may be nothing but a bundle of excuses we give to rationalize our mistakes). We become helpless victims of situations and circumstances instead of accepting accountability for our actions. Reality is difficult to deal with, and more stress-causing. Offering excuses is the easier way out.

Instead, conserve your energy for understanding the valuable lesson held in the feedback. Respond in a manner that will help instead of hurt your future prospects. This will help in improving your overall performance. Rebuilding credibility comes easy when you take action in the required direction instead of justifying your mistakes. Instead of fighting glaring facts, accept them and move in the direction of improvement.

Push for lasting results. When faced with a setback, people often obstinately stick to their perception of reality.

Stop digging your heels and justifying what you did! Don't be hell-bent on proving yourself right or the other person wrong. Ask yourself if you'd rather be proven right or embark on the path of growth and development. If you are right, you'll end up giving up valuable learning and amazing results. You'll give up on the opportunity to better yourself. You'll only seek misleading feedback that continues to reinforce that you are right instead of offering constructive criticism in the right direction. This way, you are blocking out solutions and information that can help you in the long run.

However, if you choose growth and development, you are moving in the direction of learning and becoming a better version of yourself. By accepting accountability, you transform from being a victim to a rational individual who is keen on focusing on change and development. This is the first step towards taking responsibility, learning lessons, gaining clarity on doing things differently, and finally, producing more effective results in the future. Accept negative feedback as helpful and valuable instead of hurtful to unlock all the positives that are in store for you.

TIPS AND TRICKS FOR COMMUNICATION

The more you practice and the more skills you acquire the better off you will be when you actually find yourself in specific situations.

Body Language

When it comes to communication your body language plays a key role in bow you and your world are perceived. The first thing that you need to master is eye contact. When we talk to people if we can get them to look into our eyes we can begin to tell if they are lying, hiding something or are nervous. Eye contact is a key component in all communication.

Keeping your head raised up high. Another component in body language is how we h old up our heads. When we raise our heads up high and can look eye to eye with others it shows a level of confidence. When we have our heads hanging down low or we are moving our heads around looking at other tings in the room it is a tell sign that something isn't right.

Don't fidget with your fingers and hands. Another tell sign that you are not truthful or at least are nervous about a specific situation is how you deal with your hands. When we keep our hand still or when we are talking we move our hands we are showing emotion and confidence. If, however we are sitting still and we are tapping our fingers, biting our nails or just moving our hands up and down our clothing it shows others that we are not confident and are nervous.

There are many subtle signs when it comes to body language. When we take the time to learn all of these subtle movements and non-movements we can begin to build a picture of the internal conversations we are all having.

Participate in Conversation

Shy employees always think that their opinion won't be given importance and this fear does not let them speak up especially when they are asked to say something in a certain situation.

When you are asked to share your thoughts during the meeting, you should not hesitate to do that, no matter how hard it seems to you, because it will be a crucial step towards building your confidence and breaking the shackles for you.

You must keep one thing in mind that others are giving value to your comments or suggestions, that's why they are asking you to speak.

Adjust Your Language According to whom You are Talking To

You wouldn't necessarily talk to your friends, family, co-workers, or acquaintances all in the same way. Effective communicators are the ones who are best able to tailor their messages to their targeted audience based on whom they are speaking to. So, whenever you are preparing to have a conversation with someone, remind yourself of whom you are talking to and get in the
right frame of mind before having the discussion.

Be Concise and Specific

Practice being as concise as possible while still being able to include all the important and vital information that needs to be said or written. It may take a few practice sessions before you get the hang of it.

Being Positive

Imagine a situation where Person A is speaking in a bright, cheery manner with a smile on their face. Now, imagine Person B, who is speaking in sullen, somber tones with a serious look or frown on their face. Who would be most likely to capture your attention span? Person A of course. Always smile, because a positive attitude does make a difference, and nobody can resist a person who radiates with positive energy.

Be Mindful of Your Body Language

Effective communicators adopt an open, welcoming and inviting body language when they have a conversation with someone. Our bodies are capable of communicating without ever saying a word, so watch your body language when you are having a conversation if you want to be an effective communicator. Maintain good eye contact, never cross your arms in front of your body, smile, don't put your hands in your pockets, adopt a relaxed posture, and hold your head up high with confidence.

Keep Conversation Fillers Out

Conversation fillers here refer to the um's and the ah's that we don't even realize we are saying. Conversation fillers do nothing to help improve your communication skills. In fact, these fillers actually damper your efforts at becoming an effective communicator because too many um's and ah's makes it seem like you are unsure of yourself and what you want to say.

Say No to Distractions

Nobody likes being interrupted every few minutes when they're trying to have an important discussion. That happens all too often, especially today when mobile phones have dominated our everyday existence. To be an effective communicator, you are going to need to make an effort to put away all the distractions before you carry out a conversation, no matter who it is you may be speaking to. If you are talking to someone, they deserve your full and undivided attention. So, put the mobile phones and gadgets away and for those few minutes, just focus on the person you are talking to.

Avoid Talking Over the Person

Being a good communicator means demonstrating mutual respect for the person you are talking to. When it is their turn to communicate with you, don't interrupt them or talk over them in a louder voice that you end up drowning out their opinion. Talking over the person makes them feel disgruntled, and they will be less receptive to what you have to say in turn, so your effective communication efforts will be gone to waste.

Communicate with Patience

Everyone is different and processes information differently. Not everyone will be able to receive the information in the same manner or timeliness that you might. When communicating with other people, you need to keep that in mind and be patient in your explanation and descriptions. If they need more clarification, give it to them. Do everything that you can to make clear what it is you are trying to say. It is easy to get impatient with someone when they find it difficult to grasp immediately information that seems easy to you, but remind yourself once again that not everyone has the same level of communication. Demonstrating patience in your communication will also make the other person feel comfortable enough to ask more questions and be more receptive to what you have to say.

Prepare for Presentation

You don't have to panic whenever it's your turn to do the presentation but you should focus on things that motivate you to do it in a successful way. Tell yourself that you have to avail every opportunity that comes in your way and you have to prove your professional abilities and skills to show your superiors that you can be an asset for the organization.

Keep practicing until you feel comfortable doing it because practice is the only thing that can bring perfection in any skill.

You can also record yourself with a video camera and watch that video to judge yourself from others perspective, this way you will be able to find your weak points and work on them.

You can analyze that what standing posture will suit

you the best and overall how your body language is supposed to be, so that you look impressive while doing the presentation and everybody pays attention to what you say.

Don't Be Afraid of Fumbles

When you are in the process of improving your communication skills, you are most likely to have fumbles while you are talking at one point or the other. You don't have to be affected by this, keeping in mind throughout the conversation what happened. Just put that thing off your mind, and focus on what you are saying currently.

It's obvious that you will want to learn from your mistakes, so next time you do things in a better way without repeating them, and this is what your mind is supposed to be focused on all the time.

Listen to Your Seniors

You will start noticing a big change in your confidence and ability to communicate with excellence in any situation when you start spending more time among those colleagues whose experience can benefit you.

You can listen what they have got to share as the more you interact with them, the more you will learn from them which ultimately results in the development of your better communication skills.

Listen to the senior colleagues as much as you can because you have to be a great listener first of all, and the better you listen, the better you speak. This strategy will definitely make you successful in giving your opinion in a pompous way.

Set Small Targets

It's a great idea to monitor your progress by yourself on daily basis. You can set small targets for every day, and see whether you achieve them or not at the end of the day.

Never be aggressive or defensive

This goes back to the point of keeping our emotions in check. When we speak we tend to dig deep down into our emotional selves. When we draw from our emotions we tend to speak first rather than sit back and think of the words that come out of our mouths.

This form of communication will end up causing you more problems than they are worth. Another reason you don't want to be aggressive or defensive is that when we are calm and collected we tend to get our points across better than if we were to be combative. If you were to be in a conversation where every idea or statement that you made was challenged or told was wrong how would you react?

When we act in this fashion we will never elicit change. In fact, when we act this way people will not want to include us in the decision making process and more than likely make decisions on their own. So, when it comes to aggression and defensive attitudes you want to keep them in check. They will do more harm than good.

Don't deviate

Another thing that you will want to do when communicating with others is stay the course and don't deviate from your original thoughts. This is a huge issue when trying to get your point across to some people.

When you have a specific issue that you want to talk about you don't want to jump all around the board. For example, if you are stating that you are pro in the conversation you don't want to start making comments that are negative or go against your initial points.

When we don't deviate and are confident in our initial statements people will take our words more seriously. If, however we jump around and talk about a million different things then people will get confused and our initial meaning as well as our own train of thought will become muddled.

Be confident in your ideas

Another thing that you will want to do is make sure that you have confidence in your ideas and the points that you want to communicate. When we have an idea such as how to make a product better or how to get more customers into the store we need to make sure that we are confident in this train of thought.

Once this statement is made people will begin to process what it is that you have said and begin to form questions that will be either for that idea, against the idea or both. If you make this statement and end up having no concept on how to implement it or ways to improve upon it then people will look at you clueless and looking for some form of direction to make your idea a reality. If however you can support your idea then you will have a better chance to making it a reality instead of someone else taking over the concept and turning the idea into their own.

Use the correct communication method

When communicating with others it is your job to learn the best way the person you are talking to can process information. In many cases we only rely on verbal communications. This is typically the best way to communicate but it isn't the only way to communicate. In many situations communication through visual ques such as pictures, graphs, video and even audio will help illustrate your point and will in the long run allow people to process this information in their own way.

When we take the time to use other forms of communication we increase the likelihood that others will understand what it is we are saying and in turn can also give feedback and pointers to improving our thoughts.

End conversations with a hardy handshake

The handshake is the universal greeting and farewell that people use when starting and ending conversations. When we enter a room or meet someone for the first time we typically extend our hand out and grasp the other person's hand firmly. This sets a physical connection between the two parties. From here eye contact is engaged increasing the personal connection between the two people.

When engaging in a handshake a set amount of pressure is exerted on the hands. This is a tell sign between the two people and sometimes set the tone for dominance. For instance, if one hand exerts more pressure than the others the one with the most pressure is considered to be the more dominant person. Depending on the mental state of the individuals involved this could set the entire tone for the conversation as well as the tone for the overall relationship.

Write down everything

One of the best ways to learn to communicate as well as other tings is life is to write them down. One thing that you can do when writing things down is to write short stories. These short stories will put you in control of the actions and inactions of others.

For example, if you start with two characters in a room. In this room they have a box that needs to be opened. What you can do is start out by writing the conversation that each person would have. You can then jump into writing about the inner dialogue that each person is having. You can talk about what they are thinking compared to what they actually say. You can talk about their body language, their fears, hopes and desires.

At the end of the story you can conclude it with different endings. For example, could the box be a birthday or Christmas present. Who give the present to this individual and what is their relationship status?

When we write down these stories we can begin to train our brains to react and even anticipate actions and events that may occur in real life. If you are having trouble coming up with a story or a plot just go back to a time in your life where you had a conversation with someone that didn't go well. Start writing down what happened exactly how it occurred in real life and then make marks in the story where you wish you had made a different decision or choice. From there you can flesh out the story and make it your own. Then the next time you find yourself in this situation or a similar situation you can craft the real life story to reach your intended outcome.

HOW TO DEVELOP GOOD COMMUNICATION SKILLS?

In order to develop healthy communication skills, it is crucial that you become ready to completely shed off your old skin and turn into a new person altogether. Sticking to your old self won't help since communication requires you to open up and spread out as much as possible.

Everyone hears, very few listen. The first step to a good communication is listening. It's only when you hear the other party that you grasp how to respond. Blabber on your own track and you fail to be a communicator from the very start.

Speak

Ever since man's stopped using sign language to communicate, speaking has dominated his usage of tongue to convey information. What would you call speaking? Using words to send relevant data? Speaking has evolved into more than a mere sending of words.

Speaking is the use of tongue to convey emotions, intentions and information to other people. It helps you make others understand what you want, know or feel. If it were not for speaking, humans would have still used hand gestures to show they are hungry, sleepy or horny. Just imagine such a scenario.

Speaking opens not only your mouth but also your mind. The action of speaking requires and pushes you to think. Thinking is an activity that keeps you engaged mentally. When you think, you naturally develop and sharpen your mind. Your mind opens shut doors to let you think and speak. You start accepting new ways to form opinions and to put them out for others to see.

There is no limit to your wings of imagination. You start exploring new dimensions and seeing better ways to perceive people. Basically, you change your personality in such a manner that others notice changes in you. Speaking therefore, opens you up. It removes fetters from your development and lets you witness the best you can achieve. Speaking is an art, which when mastered, covers almost more than half of your communication skills.

Mind your body language

Body language could be defined as a combination of all those physical activities that you unintentionally perform that depicts your intentions and emotions. The amount of communication you perform by your body language is almost as equivalent as the amount you perform by what you say.

Communication isn't always vocal. It assumes different forms like eye movements, talking style, hand gestures and general hand movements. Body language is a good way to avoid using words and ensuring quick sending of messages. It's easy and smart to communicate without putting any special efforts into it. Talking is good, sure, but what if you had better options to convey information? Body language is the answer.

Spice up

Everyone speaks. But those who leave an impression behind on their listeners' minds are the ones remembered. Simply constructed sentences and casually picked up words hardly do justice to a speaker's image. When you do not infuse life into your words, you fail to impress those listening. By life, I mean excitement, appeal and class. When you make your conversations funny, witty and sarcastic, you open new doors of possibilities.

So how do you go about spicing up your conversations? If there's a possibility for a fun angle being added to your sentences, go for it. Do not hesitate to imagine well and imbibe the said imagination into your words. Cleverly selected words have more magic than casually said ones.

Briefness is another character that elevates your conversation's worth. The briefer your sentences, more the impact you leave behind. A study found that shorter sentences have more conviction powers than longer ones. When you wrap up your conversations with short sentences, you allow the other party to think back-something that is not possible with long sentences. When you allow the listeners to think upon what you have just said, they realize it makes sense.

On the contrary, when you do not allow such time, they assume you are either bluffing or trying to dominate the proceedings. Shorter sentences therefore, enhance your impact as a communicator.

Sarcasm is a trait not everyone possesses. It is the rare quality to whiplash someone without them knowing that you have just owned them. The quality of sarcasm is a funny way to get back to those opposite you. If you master the quality well, you could enter into any argument blind-folded. Though seen as a last resort in a debate, it serves a great deal when you want to make the opposite party regret locking horns with you. Being a good communicator requires the inculcation of the characteristic of sarcasm in your skills-set.

Another quality that needs to be possessed by you in order for you to turn into a good communicator is humor. Humor never fails to entertain listeners. If you have this trait on your side, you not only end up making your point but also make the audience laugh. The purpose of conveying through a message is accompanied by the incentive of a funny laugh. However, when you communicate you should guard against excessive or negative humor. Humor in excess dilutes the conversation and shifts the direction from your conversation to fun. The very purpose of having a conversation is defeated. Negative humor is that which offends race, gender, and similar sensitive issues. Refrain from using negative humor in your communication as it will show you in a bad light.

A good conversation involves both the parties to it-the speaker and the listener. Both the parties are accorded equal importance and neither predominates over the other. If this balance is disturbed, a conversation steers away from its purpose. Such a balance is mandatory for any conversation to achieve an ideal stage from whence it receives not only acknowledgement but also applause from the audience.

When an already perfect conversation is infused with things like fun, sarcasm, witticism and intellect, the impact such a conversation has on its listeners is huge. A bland and dry conversation is only informative. But a conversation that is infused with the mentioned traits does more than informing. It keeps the parties excited and informed. It makes them crave for more and never bores them throughout the conversation. The communication you perform this way is an ideal one.

Read

Reading is a habit that when inculcated in a human reaps him numerous benefits. When you read, you explore the world. New doors of shining experiences get open and you start seeing things through other people's perspectives. You get yourself familiar with people, their views and their angle of thinking. Reading familiarizes you with images that you never thought would be possible.

The habit of reading is vital to be infused at a young age. When children are taught to not just learn reading but also keep continuing it, they have a particular thing to return to. With age, this habit turns into a hobby and kids start exploring various genres. Be it fiction or autobiographies, they cannot keep their hands off books in general. They squeal upon coming across a bookshop and spend all their pocket money on buying books. The art of buying second-hand is more pronounced in your kids than it may be in you. Tender minds are like clean slates. Whatever you write on them will stay for a long time in their lives. When you introduce kids to such a healthy habit, you essentially push them towards being a good communicator.

Socialize

When you meet new people, you pick up their stories

and experiences. Everyone has learnt a lot of lessons from their lives. When they share it with others, they allow them to become a part of their stories. By becoming a part of their stories, you learn the lessons they learnt. The very essence of communication is that it is to be facilitated by at least one party. When you are the one doing it, you need to pick up the social courage to do it. If you shy away from social company, you are killing any chances of socializing, and hence by extension, communication.

Socialization is the art of mingling with the society. It requires you to gel well with those who are not a part of your family. You may know your family members very well but that's not the case with others.

Upon socializing, you choose to allow others the chance to know you and get familiar with your experiences. Such discretion in social gathering opens your dam-gates of mind. You no longer shut yourself down in your room getting busy with online social networking. You start attending social gatherings and mingle with other members of the society. Those who didn't know you before start getting familiar with you. Socialization is a necessary performance to be performed by anyone who wishes to develop his communication skills.

The very act of communication requires that there has to be one audience. Who better a candidate than society? The little talks you have in a kitty party, the jokes you enjoy sharing in your club's meetings, the interesting people you meet in your tennis club; it all helps your communication skills in this way or other.

Society is the base of communication. If communication were bacteria, society would be its petri-dish where it's cultivated and grown for further spreading. If it were not for the society, communication would have developed as a skill. It is only when we start mingling with others that the art of communication gets pronounced.

Keep improving your vocabulary

It is a common experience that we do not find the right words for the right things. This happens because of a neglected or unimproved vocabulary. Vocabulary is the human storehouse of words that one uses while expressing himself orally.

This oral mishap happens because we either haven't been practicing on our vocabulary or it's been that redundant since the start. Vocabulary is a like a pet; you just don't stop at buying a dog; you have to get it vaccinations, feed it pedigree and look after its bath schedules from time to time. You might also have to train him to poop at the right place!

Your vocabulary is nothing very different from a pet dog. You have to train your vocabulary from time to time in order to make sure it's functioning smoothly. To ensure kits efficiency you must keep adding words to it. Not just addition, deletion is important too. There are always words that get scrapped or out of usage with time. Keep modifying your vocabulary to meet your situations.

Always have a dictionary at hand. These days, you also have an option for downloading an online dictionary that can be accessed even when you are offline. There are many applications for smart phones that teach you one word a day.

A good vocabulary is that one which always has backups stored. A word has not only synonyms but also antonyms. Get yourself familiar with all the synonyms and antonyms of a new word that you learn. It also helps to know the origin of the word, but it's not mandatory. Apart from having backed up words, it's really worth it to know the minute difference between two similar sounding words. Here's a little example to explain this:

There are two words that sound strikingly similar and are yet brilliantly different from each other. 'Alone' and 'Lonely' are often used interchangeably by people who do not pay much attention to the intricacies of their vocabulary. However, a real communicator who knows better than to mix up his words would know the real difference.

The word 'alone' is used in situations where you need

to describe physical isolation. When a person is only physically single, he's alone. But the word 'lonely' is used to talk about situations that describe a person who is only mentally single. When you feel lonely, you are likely to be sad. But when you are alone, you are only single in terms of physical company. Sadness is more likely to happen in the latter case.

A good communicator always knows the exact difference between two similar sounding words. This saves you from social embarrassment.

Vocabulary used to have a very narrow definition attached to it. The old description had the meaning of vocabulary to imply something that consisted of only words. However, a more liberal form of definition says that an ideal vocabulary is more about than just words. A healthy vocabulary should always include things like idioms, wit and other necessary literary devices.

Communication skills require the application of not just your word knowledge but also the optimum accompanied action. The tone with which you speak, the manner which you adopt while speaking and the kind of impression your words leave behind; they all add up to develop a good vocabulary.

HOW TO BE A CHARISMATIC CONVERSATIONALIST AND INCREASE YOUR SOCIAL CHARISMA

How can you build an irresistible social persona or magnetic social power? What are the traits that differentiate ace communicators from regular ones? What are the unspoken, hidden x-factors that reality show judges look for in contestants?

Make others feel special

Some of the world's most powerful communicators understand the importance of making other people feel special. They earn a loyal following based on their ability to make others feel valued, cherished and great about themselves. Charismatic communicators know how to hold a compelling conversation by concentrating on other people's life, passions, and interests. They demonstrate a genuine interest in people. People seldom forget how you make them feel even if they don't remember what you did or didn't do for them. Use this to your benefit through every given opportunity to make people feel special about them! Speak about their strengths, encourage/hail them publicly, and highlight their positives – basically, place them on a pedestal to increase your own likeability and charisma.

Express discomfort or have tough conversations with ease

At times, we have no choice but to have difficult, uncomfortable conversations with people or communicate with difficult people. The manner in which you handle these potentially conflict-laden and tricky situations contribute to our overall popularity. You don't need to go guns and daggers after people if you disagree with them.

There can be disagreements and conflicts between people all the time in personal, professional and social settings. However, prevent them from snowballing into something bigger.

When you have something uncomfortable to say to the other person or discuss it with them, say something like, "Jill, I need to speak to you about something that has been troubling me for long. This way you are assuming responsibility for experiencing a particular feeling rather than accusing the other person. When you begin your sentence in the manner mentioned above, the other person immediately lowers his/her defenses and becomes more open and receptive to what you are saying.

Adapt to multiple communication styles

This is as important for leaders as for people seeking more harmonious interpersonal relationships. Adapting to different communication styles in integral to the process of a being an effective communicator and speaker.

Likewise, when you are communicating with baby boomers, you'll use a different communication approach than if you are communicating with Millennials. While baby boomers are more open to personal, face to face communications, Millennials may prefer emails, instant messaging and video conferencing.

As a leader or communicator, you'll be required to tune in to the preferences, personalities, demographics and communication style of your team members or audience. Even in personal encounters, you may have to adapt to your partner's or friend's communication style to build more harmonious and fulfilling relationships.

Be a smart observer

Some of the best conversationalists and most effective communicators I know are the ones who notice and talk details. Ever wondered by fiction authors and professional scriptwriters weave such wonderfully imaginative stories, concepts, and ideas? Artists, poets, writers and other creative professionals are brilliant observers. They skillfully notice things and people around them to create ideas, images, and characters. They are pros at observing and absorbing diverse situations while giving it their own interpretation. These are the people who will offer detailed compliments or comment on a fascinating wall artifact or jewelry piece someone's wearing at a party. They will quickly notice people's accents and start talking to them about it. Their conversations are based on detailed and interesting observations. It comes with practice. Start being more observant and conscious of people and things around you! Give yourself a clear conversation edge by noticing small details that a majority of people overlook. You will come across as an exciting, creative and interesting conversationalist who is in sync with the listener.

Offer interesting, detailed an exciting insight into your conversation. Avoid speaking or talking regarding expected, basic or simplistic. Don't state the obvious. Instead of talking about the latest breaking news that people must've heard a hundred times by now, offer your own unique take or view of it to make the interaction more memorable. Keep some trivia handy or know interesting/fun facts at the back of your hand, and pepper your conversation with it. I also like reading about interesting research in the field of human behavior and psychology, which is almost always a winner. People enjoy talking about psychological research, self-help topics, and behavioral patterns. Pop psychological insights also make for an interesting conversation topic, which appeals to a majority of people.

Always offer one or two useful takeaways

Offer people something to take back irrespective of whether you are addressing a single person or a group of people who are struggling with an issue. Always end your talk or conversation with a couple of actionable, practical and realistic takeaways can be applied in their daily life. It will increase the value of your conversations, and make interacting with you more desirable.

Avoid talking to people in a patronizing or sermonizing manner when they share an issue or problem with you. I know plenty of people who talk down to others or imply that they've been really foolish to get into xyz situation. Don't do that. Talking down to people never helps. You'll seldom win people by making them feel miserable about themselves. Instead, empathize with them, and offer practical solutions. Unsolicited opinions and sermons serve no purpose. Give them an actionable piece of advice they can start implementing immediately. At the end of the conversation, they should have a valuable and doable solution.

Employ the power of personal stories

Charismatic communicators know how to make themselves irresistible, likable and relatable by narrating personal experiences and anecdotes. They make their interactions even more interesting, fascinating and personal by sharing their own stories as examples or to demonstrate to the other person how they've been in a similar situation. It makes them come across as more identifiable and relatable. This technique also helps create a common foundation for establishing deeper and more meaningful relationships with people.

Confidence is the key factor

Confidence and self-assuredness don't equal arrogance. It is being comfortable in your skin and having faith in your capabilities. Keep a polite, well-mannered, courteous and assertive stance while communicating with people.

Develop the art of speaking with conviction. If you want to develop greater confidence, stand in the front of the mirror while talking. This helps you realize how you come across to others while talking. You'll also identify areas of improvement to boost overall confidence.

Confidence is a huge component of charisma. Also, it is an evolving trait. It's a work in progress. If something is destroying your confidence or making you feel inadequate about yourself, pin it down. There can be some things from speech to hair to knowledge. Focus on growing your positives, and improving your weaknesses. Boost your personal appearance, skills, posture, and knowledge to make you feel wonderful about yourself.

Use humor to your advantage

Ask the next 10-20 people you interact with what makes a person highly irresistible to them, and a majority will most likely respond with a fabulous sense of humor. Who doesn't like people who make them laugh! People with a wonderful sense of humor are attractive, popular and much sought after everywhere. They have people hooked to everything they say and do. There is an unmistakable charisma surrounding them. Ever thought about why Oprah Winfrey is among the wealthiest and most sought-after television/media personalities? She is a wonderful blend of humor, honesty, and empathy (one of the most killer combinations when it comes to winning people).

Make other people laugh, and activate their feel-good hormones. You will always have a solid edge over others if you can make people smile or laugh. Have you observed how you are likely to buy from salespeople who make you laugh? Contrast this with people who simply go on and on about a product's features in a tiring monotone. We all know how men/women with a totally dig-worthy sense of humor have the most attractive girls/boys flocking to them. They are the subject of absolute envy. Start developing a sense of humor today by reading more, watching funny content, and coming up with your own creative lines (think about the most hilarious thing you can say in any situation).

Be genuine and authentic

This should be understood, but it's funny how many

get it completely wrong. They put on pretenses, and come across as highly obnoxious and preposterous to others. Do not pretend to be something you clearly aren't.

While it alright to fake a little confidence to be able to be practice being more at ease in social relationships and develop greater self-assuredness in social situations, don't try to project something you are not just to be popular. Once the mask wears off, people will discover the truth and stay miles away from you. Make a conscious increase your charisma, become more influential and develop a more persuasive communication style, while still being true to yourself. Stay natural, authentic and trustworthy. You should come across genuine to other people to inspire their trust and increase your likeability factor.

TECHNIQUES TO MASTER
EVERY COMMUNICATION

Here are 10 communication techniques to master, each is just as important in personal and social life, as well as at work or outside the office with your colleagues. By learning these techniques by heart, you will be able to quickly connect to anyone, earn their respect, and gain influence.

Be Friendly.

People are drawn to signs of friendliness. People with a smiling face and pleasing personality always have an edge in every communication. Friendly people bring an automatic wave of calmness; they put people at ease, enabling them to open up and speak freely. This is a must, especially when your aim is to practice your communication skills. People who are ready to listen and share will make everything easier for any speaker.

Never sound like a fool.

Think before you speak. Be prudent enough to think first before talking about something. People who never filter their words are often considered reckless. It is important to always know what you are talking about. And even if you know what you are talking about, make sure that you are sensitive enough to tell if what you are saying will produce a negative reaction among your listeners. People with good communication skills often leave their listeners inspired and feeling great.

Clear as crystal.

If you want to excel in communication, find ways to convey your message in a brief and clear manner. Avoid being indirect as it would only confuse your listeners. You would not want to leave your audience bewildered and asking what it was you really meant.

Too much is always bad.

Be concise, less is always good when conveying your message. Never attempt to sound "intellectual" by injecting too many words. Also, never use jargons and difficult words just to project an impressive image. No matter how many words you use, how many sentences, if your listeners are not able to absorb what you are saying, then you fail as a speaker.

Be Authentic.

Integrity, humility, and honesty are very important when conveying something. People have the natural ability to detect inconsistencies in what others are saying, so never pretend just to win over your listeners.

Be confident.

Humility is never about the lack of confidence. On the other hand, humility is about knowing what you are capable of and knowing your limitations. The self-awareness you get from humility should be enough to boost your confidence. Speak with a conviction that you know what you are saying; use appropriate tone to convince them of your honesty and sincerity. Make eye contact to draw them to you and the things you want to say to them.

Body language.

Hand gestures and facial expressions will always make it easier for your listeners to understand what you are saying. So, use them to your advantage and eliminate the chances of being misunderstood. Your body language will put real meaning to the words you are using.

Tone is everything.

Whether you are face to face with someone or you are speaking to somebody over the phone, your tone plays a big part in perfecting your communication skills. Words are naked without the proper tone. Tone gives your words the authority they need to be absorbed by your listeners. Over the phone, tone dresses you up in the mind of the listener.

Positive scripting.

Words are powerful. With the right vocabulary and the right tone, you can make other people feel better. Practice using positive words in conveying your thoughts and emotions even when telling something about a challenging experience. In doing so, people around you will always feel happy when with you.

Listen.

It is only natural to be drawn to someone who is a great listener. Even when you are not connecting with anyone, people will remember you if you take this technique by heart, they may even contact you when they need to talk to someone. It will be a huge compliment on your part when someone contacts you and invite you for a quick chat. This shall be a clear sign that you are moving forward in your quest to acquire good communication skills.

Follow these techniques and you will never go wrong. When your listeners are able to feel good when talking to you, they will open up to you more and share. In return, they themselves can make your job as the speaker a lot easier. The aim of the techniques above is to make sure that you always establish a good rapport with your listeners. With enough practice, you will find out that your very positive presence is enough to draw people around you.

APPLYING COMMUNICATION SKILLS WHEN COMMUNICATING WITH STRANGERS

However much you detest it, meeting and interacting with strangers is an integral and inescapable part of your life. We come across people we know nothing about in our everyday life. The good news is there are some smart tricks on hand to get strangers to like you immediately.

Use Their Name Multiple Times

Strangers don't really expect you to use their names as soon as they introduce themselves to you or are introduced to you by a third person. Plus, people are naturally wired to adore the sweet sound of their names (narcissism pays). Once you get to know someone's name, use it a few times during the conversation naturally.

Don't overdo it or it'll come across as fake. I always notice when I address customer service representatives with their names a few times during the call, they become even more eager to help. The person invariably feels a sense of connection or friendliness towards you. The icy vibes of being strangers thaw a bit and he/she becomes more familiar when they address you by your name.

Also, when you repeat a person's name more than once, the chances of remembering it increase. This can save you the embarrassment of forgetting names (and permanently burying your chances of being liked by the person).

Smile and Maintain Eye Contact

This one's a no-brainer all the way. Smiling a universal expression of linking or opening up to someone. Offer strangers a genuine and warm smile to increase feelings of familiarity. It makes you come across as more approachable, amicable and friendly. Plus, it establishes a more positive tone for future interactions. The tiny act of smiling leads the brain into releasing chemical hormones that make you feel happier as a person. This way, you'll enter into an interaction feeling friendlier, happier and more positive, which invariably makes you more likable.

Eye contact is a universal expression or signals of confidence, transparency, honesty, and genuineness. More than 50 percent of our communication happens visually.

Use the Head Tilt

The head tilt is a wonderful non-verbal way to communicate your interest to a stranger or to get a stranger to like you. This communicates subconsciously to the other person that you aren't a threat to them because you are exposing your carotid artery. It is the primary artery that supplies blood to your brain, and any damage to this artery can lead to instant death or permanent brain damage. By exposing this region of your body, you are signaling to the stranger that neither are they a threat to you nor are you a threat to them. You are non-verbally setting the stage for a non-threatening relationship.

Use Empathetic Statements

Empathetic statements help retain the focus on another person, thus making you come across as more likable. People generally like the focus to be on themselves and not others. They feel wonderful when they are the center of attention. Don't parrot their statements for it may come across as patronizing or condescending. Rephrase what they've said while keeping the focus on them. The standard formula for creating empathetic statements should be, "So, what you are feeling or saying is….."

This immediately makes them the focus of the conversation. Something like, "I understand how you are feeling." The idea is to always have the other person as the focus of your conversation. This basic formula seldom goes wrong when it comes to being liked by strangers.

Ask for Favors

I know this seems amusing and even counterintuitive. I mean if you asked someone for a favor and they did fulfill it, you'd like them, right? However, Ben Franklin noticed that each time he asked co-workers for a favor, they liked him more than when he didn't ask for favors. This can work for strangers too when it comes to breaking the ice and opening up people towards you. "Oh you work for XYZ Company; I was really hoping to get the contact details of the marketing manager for a brand association or tie-up. I'd be really nice if you could help me with their contact details."

When someone does a favor, they feel great about themselves, and if you ask a person for a favor you are helping them feel wonderful about themselves. This goes a long way toward increasing your likeability quotient. It makes the person who is doing the favor bigger or focus of attention, which makes them feel good. However, don't overdo when it comes to asking people favors just so they like you more. Asking for too many favors will have people running in the opposite direction.

Talk to Strangers All the Time

If you'd given me this piece of advice a few years ago, I'd freak out. I mean I can go around stranger hopping, having happy conversations with strangers. I mean this goes against everything we've been taught since childhood about staying away from strangers.

Don't be bothered too much about making a glowing first impression. They are trying to make you like them as much you are trying to get them to like you, so it is an even game. Don't overthink or over-strategize how to approach people. Just be natural, friendly and approachable. Focus on everything that can be controlled, including the direction of the conversation.

Keep Your Body Language Open and Approachable

Did you know that strangers form an impression about you within the first four seconds of seeing or meeting you? The first four seconds are highly crucial when it comes to forming an impression about unknown people. This means the person will form an opinion about you even before you probably say anything at all! The onus in such cases is on your non-verbal signals or body language. Keep your body language relaxed and open.

Of course, actions speak louder than words. They work on a very subconscious and primordial level. Keep your gestures, posture, expressions, leg movements etc. more approachable. This can help determine on a subconscious level whether strangers view you as an open and receptive person. Your body language will determine whether a person likes you or not, irrespective of what you say.

Keep your palms and arms open if you want to come across as a more approachable and receptive person.

This makes you more likable to strangers because you come across as someone who is high on energy, expression, and enthusiasm. You come across as a more expressive, animated and articulate person. People respond more positively to people who are animated in their gestures.

Offer Sincere and Specific Compliments

Instead of telling someone how wonderful their outfit is, you can say the cut looks superb on them or you love the way the fit of the attire. Similarly, instead of telling someone that he/she is a good speaker, pick out bits and pieces from the conversation that you really enjoyed. Another favorite is, instead of saying, "you are beautiful" or "you have lovely eyes" say something like, "The color of your eyes is beautiful" or "you have a very soulful pair of eyes." Start with a warm smile, maintain eye contact, and then compliment them on their eyes. It works wonders!

Applaud them for the humor they used in the speech or their powerful vocabulary. Making the compliment specific makes you come across as more genuine than a plain flattery person. Compliments are a great way to get into the good books of strangers.

Make People Laugh

For all the communication tips I give people, this one probably tops the list when it comes to breaking the ice with strangers. People will adore you if you make them laugh. It is no secret that salespersons who make their potential customers laugh score high sales figures or customer service representatives who make customers laugh score high on customer satisfaction.

Ensure that you don't crack offensive jokes or resort to humor related to sensitive issues such as religion, race etc. Keep it clean, intelligent, simple and healthy. People are generally stressed, exhausted, and bored with their daily grind. When you resort to humor, you lighten up their day by making them laugh. It gives them a break from a mundane existence which makes you endearing to them. If they tell you they are having a tough day or were late for work today, give it a more light-hearted-spin. This will transform their sullen mood and make them more receptive to a conversation.

HOW TO COMMUNICATE WITH PEOPLE TO BUILD FRIENDSHIPS

Friendship, however, is incredibly important. Friends help relieve stress, make you happier, give advice, and just generally make your life better. How do you make lasting friendships like that?

Choose Carefully

You cannot be friends with everyone. Well, maybe you could, but it is not recommended. It is best to remain acquaintances with people until you have time to 'test the waters' and see how you feel about the other person. If you feel awkward or out of place, this is probably not the person you are looking for. If you are relaxed and feel as though you are able to be yourself around this person and speak easily, then you have found a good candidate.

Honesty

The key to any relationship is to be honest and genuine. The same goes for friendship. You can't be good friends with fake people. Don't be afraid to open yourself up. Always speak the truth and be authentically yourself. When you share stories, allow your new friends to see the emotions the story causes, lay yourself out there. Does this open you up for heartache and hurt? Yes, in a way, but it also lays down a foundation of trust and compassion decent people will not be able to deny. Give your friend compliments, it is totally okay. Also, be thankful when they give you compliments, but remember to be humble and stay grounded.

Don't Be Afraid of Silence

When speaking of communication, people assume that means you have to actually speak. This is not so. We have all heard or experienced the so-called awkward silence. The beauty of a true friendship is that there is no awkwardness in the silence. You are able to sit together and just do things quietly without feeling like you should get up and go. This kind of silence speaks volumes about trust and mutual respect.

Don't Step Down

If for some reason you and your friend find yourselves at odds, do not back down. Never walk away from an argument. Take the time to calmly make your side known, careful to keep your tone level and your words small. Make clear what the problem is and how you feel about it. Then, be sure to offer your friend the same in return. Be an active listener, look them in the eye, use your body language to show that you are interested in the conversation, and do not interrupt.

Communication is a useful tool in more professional relationships as well. You can use these skills to market and network yourself to the general public in order to boost your business and get your name out.

MAKE YOUR CONVERSATIONS UNIQUE AND MEMORABLE

We hold so many conversations in our daily lives with family, colleagues, business associates, acquaintances, bosses, neighbors, and even strangers. Most of them are soon forgotten; then there are those that linger in our minds for a long time. What separates the common conversation from truly great ones? Here's how to have unique conversations:

Full concentration

We often hold conversations when also concentrating on something else; a task, TV or phone. Multitasking has become a standard operating procedure. By the end of the conversation, neither party can outline what was said in the conversation. Make your conversation unique by paying full attention. Maintain a steady 70 – 80% eye contact. It will be a refreshing change for people that are used to being listened to just partially. If you're a fan of meditation, we call this listening mindfully. Mindfulness basically refers to living at the moment and enjoying all aspects of it. When you listen mindfully, you're attentive to every detail. The speaker will feel valued, appreciated and cared for, and will have no problem opening up.

Compliments

Throw in a genuine kind word here and there. It helps break the ice and places the discussion on a positive stand. As the conversations go on, you can identify more areas that deserve a compliment. Let's say people are talking about their careers. Somebody in the group mentions that they work for a particular real estate company. You happen to know that (remember what we said about staying informed?) that company is undertaking a massive project in the neighboring county. You can congratulate the speaker on the work 'they' are doing. Let the compliments be brief; just a sentence or two. The effect is still outstanding. The receiver feels noticed, appreciated and validated. With such a lifted spirit, the conversation is bound to be remembered for a long time.

Balance speaking and listening

This is a balance that is so often lacking, yet even those responsible for it could be doing so subconsciously. There are those self-absorbed people that will go on a monologue while everybody else is quiet. Such a scenario may even be thought of as a positive thing; 'they're all letting me speak since I'm the expert.' Unless you're giving a speech to an audience, dominating the dialogue as such is inappropriate. You risk coming across as proud and arrogant. However well you know the subject matter, or how good your oratory skills are, give the others an opportunity to speak.

You may be on the other side of the coin, where you hardly say anything in conversations. You're the quiet listener. Anything wrong with this approach? Absolutely. A conversation is a team effort. Whether you're engaging one other person or a group of people, all parties should participate. When you remain silent, the interlocutor(s) are inwardly trying to figure out why. Is the conversation boring? Are you not interested in the topic of discussion? Or are you devoid or content to contribute? See? You're taking their mental energy away from the conversation and tasking them with the burden of trying to interpret your actions. All this can be avoided if you contribute periodically, and facilitate a truly memorable conversation.

Steer the conversation

Once you break the ice with small talk, don't dwell there for long. Small-talk is unfulfilling and gets people easily bored. Pick cues of the interlocutor's interests from the conversation. From there, direct the conversation towards a deeper issue. From casual comments about the speakers in a conference, you can ask a question like, 'what do you expect the presenters will address this afternoon?' You can then talk about your expectations for the meeting and other relevant matters concerning the event.

Similarly, a random comment about sleeping in for the weekend can be turned into a more meaningful conversation about rest, unwinding, working hard vs working smart, work-related stress and so on. A deep conversation makes a lasting impression.

Use technology

We have stated before that you should avoid your gadgets when having a conversation, but isn't there an exception to every rule? If you've tried all means and the conversation still ends up stalling, you can compromise a bit. Refer to something interesting, informative, funny or relevant that you can come across online. Say something like; 'have you watched this documentary on the long-term effects of these Chinese loans?' Go ahead and steam the clip from your phone or laptop. It does not have to belong. And if it is, you don't have to watch the whole of it.

As the people turn their attention to the video, you will have time to catch a breath. Trying to keep a conversation going can be draining, you know. The conversation will then resume on a new angle. People will now be giving their views on what they just watched. Others could take the queue and also share the content they have on their gadgets. You all can then have something in common to speak about.

Exit politely

Sometimes, even after your best effort, the conversation cannot seem to gain traction. You do not have to suffer endlessly. You can excuse yourself. Begin by summarizing what you guys last spoke about. For instance, on the video above, you can say something like, 'that is a whole lot of money to expect a third-world country to pay back in such a short time.' Then ask to leave. Thank them for their time and state that you need to leave to attend to a different matter and walk out gracefully.

COMMUNICATING WITH
DIFFICULT PEOPLE

Difficult people thrive in defying logic; or do they have a different kind of logic? It's hard to tell. While some of them are oblivious of the negative impact of their attitude, others are fully aware of the distress they cause, and it does not bother them much.

Whenever you encounter an unreasonable person, the first instinct tells you to reciprocate the exact same attitude. And why not? They started it anyway, right? This is common in a business where disgruntled customers want to give everyone a piece of their mind. Sometimes they have a legitimate concern. Sometimes not. In fact, they could be on the wrong. Perhaps you should show them that you can yell too, right?

This sounds like an easy approach. However, if you're here reading this book on communications skills, you must be interested in improving your conversation intelligence. You're keen on developing your social skills, improving empathy, learning the art of persuasion and achieving successful relationships all around. Therefore, when you encounter difficult people, you must choose to be the bigger person and deal with the situation rationally.

Don't make demands

Once a person begins being unruly, it is tempting to also shout him into submission by ordering him to keep quiet, sit down, calm down, leave and so on. But remember you're dealing with a person who is already agitated. Additional orders will only make matters worse.

Involve others

If you're certain that you're in the right, involve other people. If you're at work, call your coworkers. If not, you can involve your family, friends, and even strangers. Maybe somebody else will bring a different approach and the person will listen.

Remain calm

The problem here is not feeling angry, but letting the anger control your actions. You can control your anger (we have covered that extensively in another topic) and remain calm. Surprise the aggressor who expects you to be equally angry. He'll realize that he's the only angry one. Now that sort of embarrassing; right? He's likely to calm down on his own volition. Remaining calm also gives you the clarity of thought that you need to evaluate the situation.

Disengage

If the person totally refuses to listen, you have the right to disengage and walk away from the negativity. Say something like 'I'll talk to you later when you calm down.' If you're in your premises, have security escort him out.

Avoid violence

In worst case scenario, the person might try to hit or push you. Get away before you're provoked to fight back. You might have come across that video of a McDonald's employee who was pushed by an aggressive customer, and she then turned and attacked him viciously. She had to be restrained by her colleagues. Interestingly, the court found the customer guilty of starting the aggression. She only acted in self-defense, albeit very fiercely. This is what a moment of provocation can do to you. This can happen even to the calmest among us. Walk away quickly before your senses lead you to fight back. You can involve the police if the case meets the threshold.

Evaluate the situation

For every difficult person that you deal with without losing your calm, give yourself a pat in the back. A lesson well-learned and practiced; right? As long as you remain grounded, you emerge as the bigger person. Remember the aggressor will also be evaluating the incident later. They'll most likely feel embarrassed that they were causing all the trouble while you managed to keep calm.

Can difficult people change? Yes, they can. Yes, they

should. If you're willing to help, try to seek them out when they're in a good mood. Speak to them about their attitude and actions. They might see some sense. Give them time to go and reflect, and hopefully, they will change with time.

USE LAUGHTER TO LIGHTEN
THE CONVERSATION

Throwing in a joke or two or a bunch into a conversation makes it a lot lighter, dissipates tension and gets the listeners glued. Whether it's a corporate talk or a casual conversation, the funny fellow always gets the audience.

Some people are naturally funny, others not quite. If you fall into the second category, as most people do, you can learn to be funny. You're not trying to be a comedian; the goal here is to use humor strategically to make the conversation interesting.

Here are some guidelines in developing and using humor in your conversations.

Use it to diffuse tension

You can apply similar humor in different situations around you to melt the tension and bring the people back to a rational conversation.

This applies when you're not naturally funny and you need to put in some work. First, determine what makes you laugh. When you read or watch shows, what is it that you find funny? Is it the puns, rants or exaggeration? It is easier to develop your humor around what you find funny. Secondly, what is it that you say that gets people laughing even when you didn't intend to be funny? Is it the puns? Try working on those and using them more regularly.

Give the message priority

Don't get too excited about cracking jokes that you forget about your core content. We're using laughter here to lighten the conversation, meaning the main focus is on the conversation. If you're giving a formal presentation where you need to first write down your ideas, you don't have to include the jokes in the first draft. Dedicate the first draft to the message that you want to deliver. You can then weave in the jokes in the second draft.

Sound Natural

The jokes should blend in seamlessly into the rest of the content. Practice beforehand if you have to. Forced jokes bring in awkward moments at best. Long after you've spoken it, your listener realizes that it was supposed to be a joke. But it wasn't funny. You'll attract a chuckle at best, from a listener or two trying to be courteous. Not good at all for your impression.

Don't introduce a joke either. Just throw it in there like you're not even trying. Don't laugh at your own jokes, and definitely, don't start laughing before you crack the joke. In fact, you should look like you don't even think it's funny.

Avoid ridiculing others

Avoid poking fun directly to your listeners. Something may sound like a joke to you, while someone else hears something completely different. Make fun of things and events, not the people you're talking to. Make fun of your common challenges. It gives people the feeling of 'we're in this together.'

Teasing students over their poor performance, or employees over the company's losing streak, it not motivating them. You're just killing their spirits.

Remember to crack just enough jokes, not too many. If you're slotting in a joke after every five sentences, perhaps you should consider comedy. As long as you're engaging in normal conversation, use them only periodically. If you have mastered the art of using jokes to relieve tension, you will be better at conflict management.

DEVELOPING COMMUNICATION SKILLS

Okay, so you may not have been born with the natural gift of gab the way some people were, but there's some good news waiting for you. Everyone – yes, EVERYONE – can learn how to be an effective communicator. Thankfully, communication skills are something that can easily be developed and practiced on so you can get better progressively.

Before we begin, here is something to take note of – effective communication involves both verbal and non-verbal language. It is not just about the way that you speak, but also the manner in which you carry yourself, that makes you an effective communication overall. If you want to be successful, you are going to need to hone your skills in both of these areas.

Emphasize on Your Skills

Becoming effective at anything you want to do requires you to practice, often. The same goes for learning to communicate effectively. If you want to be successful with communicating effectively and professionally, you need to put a strong emphasis on your communication skills. Since active conversation is already a given, we are going to look at more solutions beyond this basic setting.

Take Communication Classes

Communication classes are often lead by teachers, mentors, or coaches who are effectively using communication in their own lives. As a result, they can teach you how to communicate more effectively in your own life as well.

Using communication classes as a means to begin practicing your communication skills provides you with a wonderful opportunity to have active, hands-on guidance during your learning experience. This also gives you the ability to practice with other students who are learning alongside you. For some people, learning at the same time as others makes the process a lot easier. Knowing that you are not practicing on someone who may be judging your skills means that you can eliminate the pressure and truly get some effective practice in. Furthermore, people gather at these classes specifically for the purpose of learning to communicate. As well, because you are practicing directly alongside a teacher, mentor, or coach, you can be given advice based on your specific skillset. If they recognize that you are excelling in one area but may be struggling in another area, for example, they can point this out to you and provide you with information to assist you in improving your skills.

Read as Often as You Can

Reading is another wonderful way to improve your communication skills. When you read, you gain the opportunity to learn more about how other people communicate. Through this process, you can learn about many techniques and practices that are unique to various areas of communication. For example, through actively reading you can quickly pick up on what types of words are regularly used in professional writing, versus that which are used in more casual writing pieces. This will allow you to understand what type of language is typically deemed acceptable in various circumstances. It can also help broaden your vocabulary and assist you in learning how to integrate various words into unique sentence structures.

When it comes to using reading as a tool to assist you in practicing your communication, you want to read as many different forms of written material as you can. Look toward reading newspapers, magazines, fiction and non-fiction novels, blog posts, and more. The more you diversify the materials that you use for this practice, the more you are going to be exposed to a variety of communication styles.

Practice with Other Successful Communicators

Regularly engaging in conversation with people who communicate at the level you wish to communicate at allows you to actively pick up on their skills and grow your own. When you converse with people who are already communicating at the level you desire to, it becomes easier to see how the various skills are used in practice. It also encourages you to communicate in this way so that you feel more natural and fluent in the conversation you are sharing.

There are many instances where you can find people who are communicating at the level you desire to communicate at. For example, if you intend to communicate professionally, conversing with those who are already conversing on a professional level is a great place to start. You will begin to expand your vocabulary into that unique element, as well as learn how to effectively use those new vocabulary words in active conversation. The same goes for anywhere else. The more we spend time with people who communicate and behave in a way that we desire to, the easier it is for us to integrate those new methods of communication and behavior into our own systems.

Use Your Skills All the Time

Lastly, if you truly want to have success with learning to communicate at a more advanced and effective level, you should be practicing your skills all the time. Those who communicate effectively do not turn their communication skills "on" or "off" from conversation to conversation. This would ultimately result in them not being able to communicate as effectively overall. Instead, they communicate with their new communication skills all of the time. Through regular and consistent practice, it becomes significantly easier to assimilate these new skills into their practice.

You should be using your new conversation skills on a

daily basis with anyone you speak with. Whether it is family, friends, cashiers, co-workers, bosses, or otherwise, communicate in the same way on a consistent basis. When you do this, you will gain plenty of opportunity to expand your practice and skills. This will result in you communicating more effectively consistently, and with ease. There will be no considering "how" to communicate between person to person, because you will do it the same way every time: effectively and professionally.

Keep Things Simple

When we attempt to integrate difficult skills into our communication strategies, it can create a world of distraction and chaos. Trying to recall difficult strategies and integrate them in active practice is challenging, especially when you are likely already communicating beyond your present level of experience. Keeping things simple is necessary if you want to communicate effectively with other people.

When you attempt to add too many complex strategies and skills in place at any given time, effectively communicating can be challenging. Not only will you struggle to recall the many different strategies you are attempting to integrate, but your audience will also struggle to understand what you are attempting to communicate. There is no need for communication to be a difficult, complex, or over-done process. In fact, the very opposite tends to work far better.

Think about it: if you are trying to learn to communicate more effectively and with greater professionalism, stumbling over your words and taking several moments between sentences to attempt to recall all of your unique strategies will be a struggle. You are likely going to struggle to integrate any communication skills because you are attempting to integrate too many to begin with. Furthermore, the majority of people do not communicate at a complex level. Attempting to communicate with your audience with an advanced level of complexity may result in them becoming confused and not thoroughly understanding what it is that you are attempting to say. Most people like things straight forward and to the point. Keeping it clean and simple like this ensures that they know exactly what they are being told and prevents miscommunications from happening. Attempting to interpret too many different, potentially conflicted pieces of communication can become stressful and will result in both you and your audience being out of sync.

Simplifying the process means that you choose the most direct route to get to your point. You keep your words clean, simple, and clear. You directly tell your audience what it is that you are trying to communicate, and you use the best vocabulary to communicate your point perfectly. In doing so, it becomes significantly easier for them to understand what it is that you are trying to express to them. It also prevents you from getting confused in the process of actually trying to express it to begin with. Ultimately, what happens is that the conversation remains clear and consistent, and everyone understands what the purpose of the conversation is.

Be Clear with Your Message

Expanding off of the practice of simplicity, it is important that you are always clear with your message. Before you attempt to articulate yourself to someone else, know exactly what it is that you want to say. Being clear with your message ensures that everything you say is accurate to what you are thinking and feeling. You are able to then express yourself effectively, efficiently, and with professionalism.

Self-Awareness

Understanding your message comes from having a level of self-awareness that allows you to truly comprehend what your message is. For many of us, poor communication skills start from within. When we are unclear about what it is that we are truly feeling or thinking, it becomes significantly harder for us to communicate these feelings and thoughts to other individuals. Learning how to truly decipher the meanings of our thoughts and feelings and how they translate into what we want to share with the other person is important.

When you are communicating with someone, before you share your message, take a moment to think about what it truly is. Often, the initial thoughts or feelings we have may not be clear or in alignment with what it is that we are actually attempting to convey to the other person. For example, in some situations we may be elated that someone has offered us something, but we are not actually wanting to receive the offer, we are simply grateful that it was made. Alternatively, we may hear something and initially become angry, only to later realize we were actually jealous or disappointed and not actually angry. These types of confusions within our own thoughts and feelings can result in us not communicating them effectively with others, because we are not communicating them effectively with ourselves. Taking your time and learning to decipher what it is that you are truly feeling and thinking is the first step in gaining clarity around your message. Once you are clear in what that is, it becomes significantly easier to share that with other people.

Know Your Perspective

In addition to knowing what you are feeling or thinking, you also need to know your perspective. The way that you can find out your perspective is to ask yourself "why" you are feeling or thinking the way that you are. Doing this will allow you to gain some clarity around the feelings and thoughts themselves. This will help you take them from just a thought or a feeling and turn them into an actual message. For example, "I'm angry" becomes, "I am disappointed that you would say something like that to me." This allows us to take the initial reaction or thought toward something and evolve it into a true perspective and message that we can share with the other person.

Knowing your perspective is also rooted in self-awareness. You must be self-aware enough to be able to dig deeper into the initial reactions you have so that you can translate them into a proper message. Taking your time and enforcing these self-awareness practices will ensure that you are clear on what your message is before you even attempt to share it with someone else. Being clear in yourself makes it significantly easier for you to clearly express yourself to someone else.

Express it Clearly

The key now is to take your time, choose the appropriate words, and communicate yourself in a way that clearly expresses where you are coming from, and why. Clearly sharing your message, the first time prevents you from having to repeatedly create supporting statements surrounding your message so that you can provide clarification on the various areas where you did not effectively express yourself.

Being able to clearly express your message assists in warding off unnecessary experiences that coincide with miscommunications. When we do not effectively express ourselves, we may inadvertently put someone in a position where they become defensive or upset by what we have said. We may also create confusion around our message and make it more challenging for our audience to fully understand us. Even if we end up creating clarity in the end, they will have become so confused by the beginning portion of our attempt that it will not be nearly as effective as it could have been had we expressed ourselves properly the first time. So, it is absolutely crucial that you develop clarity in your message before sharing it, and then that you share it directly and clearly.

Slow Yourself Down

Often, we find ourselves struggling to effectively communicate with others because we are attempting to communicate too quickly. All too often, we communicate by immediately and automatically expressing the first thing that comes to our minds. This is not something that we are taught, but rather it is something that we learn and continue doing because we are not taught a more effective method of communication. This very practice is responsible for us frequently saying the wrong things, expressing ourselves in a way that does not accurately reflect our thoughts, opinions or feelings, or otherwise communicating in a way that lacks clarity and efficiency. When we stop communicating automatically and begin intentionally thinking about how we wish to communicate, it becomes easier for us to express ourselves accurately to what we are actually feeling and thinking.

Give Yourself a Moment to Think

Whenever you are communicating with anyone, always give yourself a moment to think before responding to the other person. Taking this moment each time we are communicating, especially with important or sensitive topics, enables us to be absolutely certain that we are going to communicate in a way that is appropriate to how we are actually thinking and feeling.

Often, people automatically respond by immediately saying what comes to mind. These thoughts are typically unfiltered and rarely express exactly what we mean. As a result, we end up finding ourselves entering situations where we begin reconsidering the conversation later and wishing we had expressed ourselves differently. This happens because we did not take the time to accurately consider what it was that we wanted to express the first time around. When we slow down mid-conversation and use this as an opportunity to become clear and direct in our communication, the entire nature of the conversation changes. We express ourselves honestly and openly, but with tact and consideration for the others involved in the conversation. As a result, we end up finding ourselves "regretting" our expression significantly less later on because we did so effectively in the first place. Rather than wishing we had done so differently, we know that we can honestly stand behind what we said because it accurately reflected what we wanted to say.

Do Not Feel Pressured to Respond Before You Know

Although you do not want to keep the person you are conversing with waiting for an incredibly long period of time, it is important that you do not feel pressured to respond before you actually know what it is that you want to say.

The less pressure you apply to yourself to answer right away, or to take a specific amount of time before answering, the easier it will be for you to take a moment to tune in with yourself and choose an accurate answer. This may take a second, or it may take several seconds. Rarely will it last upward of about 30 seconds. That is, unless you put too much pressure on yourself. Feeling pressured to answer right away, or to wait a set amount of time before answering, makes it difficult for you to accurately tune in to what you are thinking and discover a way to communicate it. Instead, you want to eliminate the pressure. You are not required to respond immediately, nor are you required to respond after any preset amount of time. Instead, you should respond once you know what the honest thought is that you are thinking and wanting to express.

Ensure You Are Understood

Many times, miscommunication happens because we are not clearly understood by the person we are communicating with. As clearly as we may feel we have expressed ourselves, the way it is coming across to the other person may not be clear enough for them to truly comprehend what we meant versus what we said.

Ensuring that you have been understood by the person you are communicating with takes some skill, a few easy steps, and a willingness to understand that you may have contributed to the miscommunication if one does occur.

Look for Clues of Understanding

If a person understood you, there are many signs that

they may express. Nodding their head in agreement, having an open and soft body language that is receptive, and looking clearly at you are all good physical clues that the person you are talking to understands what you have said. Furthermore, they should be able to easily relay back to you what it is that you have shared with them. While not every conversation will include the other person repeating back what you said to them, the following responses they provide should clearly align with what you have shared. If they communicate back with you in a way that is very clear to what you have already shared with them and expresses no clear signs of confusion or misunderstanding, there is a good chance that what they have heard and understood is in alignment with what you have said. Other ways to ensure that the person understood what you meant may arise if you have asked a person to do something and they fulfill the duty properly based on the information you have provided them with. If the duty is fulfilled improperly, there is a good chance that the communication between you and them was not clearly articulated.

If someone does not understand what you have said to them, their clues will be completely different. Their heads may be completely still with their eyebrows pinched and a somewhat confused look on their face, expressing that they are not entirely clear on what it is that you are trying to communicate to them. They may cross their arms or grasp at one arm with their opposing hand to show that they are feeling confused and potentially nervous in the conversation. They may also tune out eventually if they feel that they truly are not getting it and that the level of communication is not improving despite them attempting to gain clarity. Verbal cues that they are not fully understanding what you have said include asking several questions to clarify what you meant, as well as providing answers that are not clearly in alignment with what it is that you meant. If the conversation warrants them repeating your message back to you, they will not be able to do so clearly because they will not be sure as to what the message actually was.

It is important that you look for these cues on the person that you are talking to.

Consider How You Have Contributed to Misunderstandings

When misunderstandings do arise, which they do from time to time no matter how well we attempt to communicate with others, it is important that we look at the situation objectively. Often, we want to quickly jump into a defensive mode and point our fingers at the other person, blaming them for the misunderstanding. It feels easier to blame them for not "getting it" than it is to blame ourselves for the fact that we may have not communicated ourselves clearly enough. Although this may make ourselves feel better in regard to who is to blame, it will not assist us in accurately and effectively clearing up the byproducts of the miscommunication itself.

First off, when we point blame at someone else it results in them also entering a defensive state of mind. This means that the miscommunication will further fester and become a complete argument or conflict between yourself and another individual. Once this occurs, the likelihood that effective and positive communication skills will be applied to this conversation drops significantly. Arguments, defensiveness, and conflict often lead to us communicating poorly as we automatically say what comes to mind as an attempt to deflect the conflict and protect ourselves from feeling hurt or attacked by the other person. When two people enter this state, the conflict becomes harder to resolve, sometimes requiring mediation for positive and effective communication to begin to be used once more.

Second, blaming the other person does not allow us to clearly identify where the communication went wrong to begin with. This is because we have quickly resorted to an argument of trying to identify who is right and who is wrong, rather than an opportunity for effective communication to ensue. As a result, we are not able to learn from the experience and therefore it becomes more likely to happen again at some point in the future.

The reality is, in these scenarios, most often it is both people who are to blame. One person failed to communicate effectively in the first place, and the second person then failed to communicate that they were not completely clear on what was being told to them to begin with. As a result, both have contributed to unclear communication practices, and both have failed to mention that they were unclear to begin with. Then, both parties take their lack of clarity with them and find themselves feeling confused and uncertain about what was gained from the conversation. They may also end up taking hurt and guilt with them from anything that may have come up during the conflict that was shared.

Use This as an Opportunity to Grow Stronger in Your Skills

Even if you are entirely to blame for the conversation resulting in miscommunication and confusion, ask for assistance in understanding why. Even if you felt you communicated clearly and it was the other person who did not explain that they were unclear with what you had said, ask for assistance in understanding why. As well, attempt to recall the conversation in your mind and see if you can pick up any clues that you may have missed in the moment that proved that the other person was not completely certain as to what was being communicated to them.

Once you have done this, you can then take the chance to identify how the conversation could have been handled differently. You can look for new opportunities to search for understanding from the person you are conversing with in the future, as well as develop new skills to avoid any mistakes you may have made that resulted in the confusion or lack of understanding. This will ensure that you grow from the unfortunate situation, rather than it becoming even more frustrating and potentially leading to further miscommunications of the same degree in the future.

Consider Your Body Language

As you already likely know, your body language plays a major role in how you communicate with other people. Your body language will either support your message, contradict it, or share an entirely different message altogether. If you want to effectively communicate with other people, you need to learn how you can properly consider your body language to ensure that you are communicating properly with the person you are talking to.

Our body language has the potential to contradict us in many ways, and for many reasons. As a result, we may end up inadvertently sending the wrong messages to people during our conversations. Let's explore some examples whereby your body language may result in you not effectively expressing yourself and your message to the person you are communicating with, and why these situations may happen.

Use Appropriate Styles of Communication

When you are communicating, it is necessary that you use appropriate styles of communication to ensure that you are being properly received by your audience. Using appropriate styles of communication will ensure that you are able to effectively share what you are thinking and feeling without miscommunications taking place. It also means that you will be able to communicate in a way that your audience can easily receive. You do not want to be communicating in the wrong style and tone for your audience, or you may disrupt your effective communication patterns and find yourself being overtaken by misunderstandings.

Learning to communicate appropriately requires you to identify your audience, communicate in alignment with them, use appropriate vocabulary, and stay on the side of caution whenever necessary. If you implement these strategies, then you will be able to easily communicate in accordance with the audience you are talking to.

CONCLUSION

Thanks for making it through to the end of this book! Effective communication doesn't have to be very difficult. It only needs the right strategies and determination to master communication.

You are now armed with the knowledge and the skills that you need to become a more effective communicator. The next step is to apply the techniques that you have learned in this book and start practicing them in your everyday life and in your workplace to begin communicating more effectively and impress others with your newfound mastery of this underrated skill.

Take your new knowledge and start applying it to your life. You can certainly see that with effective communication skills, it is much easier to find happiness and success in life.

These skills take time and practice, so be sure to go easy on yourself and allow yourself the opportunity to implement them in a way that will be effective for you. It will likely result in your message becoming confusing, and your audience not truly understanding what it is that you are trying to say. Even if you do manage to finally get it across, they will likely already be too confused from everything you mentioned beforehand to actually get what you mean.

Keep this book close while working on your communication. It includes all of the information that you need to be successful. This means that it will serve as a reference now and in the future when you want to sharpen your more advanced communication skills.

ABOUT THE AUTHOR

Diego is a young entrepreneur who started his career in the real estate market about 20 years ago. Today, after attending and completing the Master in Coaching and with the title of Advanced Master Practitioner in Neuro-Linguistic Programming, he works with entrepreneurs and sportsmen to bring them to personal success. Use effective communication as a tool for achieving your goals and your clients' goals